Praise for
Who Am I Without My Partner?

Who Am I Without My Partner? packs a powerful punch of self-enlightenment. Relationships are one of the greatest sources of toxic stress thrusting men and women into endless bouts of self-destructions. Dr. Hecker gifts readers with priceless tips and tools to navigate the stormy waters encountered in any relationship. Grab a chair and sit with her as she comforts and guides you on this challenging part of your life journey.

— Pam Peeke MD, MPH, FACP
assistant professor of medicine, University of Maryland
New York Times best-selling author of *The Hunger Fix,*
Body for Life for Women, and *Fight Fat After Forty*

Dr. Hecker's powerful book gets to the heart of rediscovering yourself and your self-esteem following divorce. Her compassionate understanding of the challenges ahead coupled with her profound insights and advice are certain to make a positive impact on so many lives that might otherwise have been destroyed. Having interviewed Dr. Hecker and hearing the passion behind her convictions, I am not surprised her book is such a clear and useful roadmap toward authentic and lasting healing.

— Rosalind Sedacca,
founder of the Child-Centered Divorce Network,
author of *How Do I Tell the Kids About the Divorce?*

A must-read for those who feel emotionally drained by divorce and unsure about who they are. With its roots in psychological theory, *Who Am I Without My Partner?* impels the reader to begin anew by recognizing and understanding the dynamics of individuality before, during, and after divorce.

— Michael Mastracci,
family law and collaborative divorce attorney,
mediator, and author of
*Stop Fighting Over the Kids: Resolving
Day-to-Day Custody Conflict in Divorce Situations*

Who Am I Without My Partner?

Post-Divorce Healing and Rediscovering Your SELF

Deborah Potashnik Hecker, PhD

Who Am I Without My Partner?
Post-Divorce Healing and Rediscovering Your SELF
By Deborah Potashnik Hecker, PhD

© 2013 Deborah Potashnik Hecker

To contact Deborah Hecker, visit www.DrDeborahHecker.com.

ISBN: 978-0-615-77200-4

Library of Congress Control Number: Pending

Editing: Faith Marcovecchio, Mark Graham Communications,
www.markgrahamcommunications.com
Cover and interior design: Nick Zelinger, www.nzgraphics.com
Author photo: Lynn Stone

"What is Mine and What is Not Mine: Some Guidelines" chart in Chapter 7 from *Boundaries and Relationships: Knowing, Protecting and Enjoying the Self.* Copyright © 1993 by Charles L. Whitfield. 2010 by Alexandra Katehakis. Reprinted with permission of The Permissions Company, Inc., on behalf of Health Communications, Inc., www.hcibooks.com.

First Edition

Printed in the United States

This book is dedicated to anyone whose partnership has fallen apart and wants to heal.

Don't give up. If I can do it, so can you.
I will show you how.

ACKNOWLEDGMENTS

For Romy and Justine, whose love brought me sunshine when there was darkness.

For my Allan, whose multi-faceted, departed soul is forever in my heart.

For Faith Marcovecchio and Mark Graham, whose professional excellence consistently went above and beyond.

I thank Michael for loving me and divorcing me.

CONTENTS

Introduction

Each individual has his or her own unique version of the divorce experience. But there are certain universal thoughts, feelings, experiences, and behaviors that most divorced people share. Can you recall saying the following to yourself at some point during the process?

"I am helpless."
"I think I am going crazy."
"My life is not worth living."
"I feel dead."
"I'd like to kill my ex."
"All I do is cry."
"I don't know who I am if I am not part of a couple."

If so, you are not alone. Divorce challenges the basic sense of who you are, who you've been, and who you'll become. And yet, although millions before you have gone through it—and with the divorce rate now hovering at 50 percent, millions more will follow—being part of that large crowd doesn't necessarily make things any easier. For most, divorce is a lonely time, filled with fear and doubt.

First there are the legal entanglements. You divide assets with your soon-to-be ex, establish a new household, make custodial arrangements for your children, and, if needed, hammer out alimony payments. That can be hard enough, but it's only one face of divorce. The other side, the emotional one, can be far more complicated and difficult.

We all know that a divorce attorney is vital to the legal transition from "we" to "me." But who supports the emotional transition from being part of a couple to becoming a healthy, thriving individual?

As a therapist who specializes in divorce, I'm here to help. For more than twenty years, I've counseled thousands of men and women as they navigate the emotionally rocky waters of divorce. My patients range from people questioning whether they want to stay in the marriage to those in the midst of legal separation to men and women struggling post-divorce. Though each approaches the end of his or her marriage in a uniquely personal way, they all have one thing in common: the need to better understand what went wrong—for them as individuals as well as for the couple—and to heal and grow with that knowledge in order to have more successful relationships in the future.

There's no question we need to better understand what's going wrong with marriages. The data tell us that 41 percent of all first marriages end in divorce, 60 percent of second marriages fail, and a staggering 73 percent of third marriages don't make it.[1] There are lots of reasons given for marital breakups, from adultery to bad communication to financial difficulties. But below these difficulties lies a root cause. What is it, and how can we create a roadmap to avoid those problems, now and in the future?

* * *

---

[1] www.aboutdivorce.org.

"Though each approaches the end of his or her marriage in a uniquely personal way, they all have one thing in common: the need to better understand what went wrong—for them as individuals as well as for the couple— and to heal and grow with that knowledge in order to have more successful relationships in the future."

During my divorce twenty-seven years ago, I was in desperate need of this roadmap myself. I had been married for seventeen years to a man I thought of as the love of my life. We had two beautiful daughters, thriving professional lives, and, in my eyes, a happy, fulfilling relationship. When my husband announced to me one day that he was committed to another woman, my world was shattered. Yet to all outward appearances, I had the social, professional, and financial resources to not only survive but thrive on my own. I was a well-educated, independent woman with an established career as a psychotherapist, a loving and supportive family, and a network of therapeutic support. However, when it came to the emotional process I faced, I was so grief struck by my husband's sudden departure that I didn't know who I was anymore. It seemed to me at the time that death would be better than the situation I was in.

The tumultuous aftermath that ensued was a wake-up call for me, not only personally but also in my practice. Though I'd found a professional community to turn to, they only partially knew how to help me. Several important pieces were missing. First, there was a lack of interdisciplinary understanding of divorce that embraced both its legal and emotional aspects—the transition from being part of a couple to being successfully divorced has as much to do with exercising emotional intelligence as it does legal smarts. There was also a gaping inattention to the inevitable question divorcing people ask themselves: "Who am I apart from my marriage?"—a question that focuses on attachment as well as loss. In therapy, though my psychologist understood the need to grieve my devastating situation, way too much time was spent on blaming my husband (as much as he deserved it) and not enough on facing and identifying my underdeveloped Self. That had been the true impasse to creating a better and more successful marriage. What was missing was the concept of developing my "I" apart from the enmeshed boundaries I had unconsciously formed with my husband, that messy gray area where it's hard to tell where you end and your partner begins. In short, I needed to accept greater responsibility.

It didn't take long before I began to make the connection between my experience and those of my divorcing or divorced patients. A common picture began to take shape of unpartnered people unsure of who they were without their spouse. The advice many divorcing people receive of "Just move on" was simply unfathomable—to my patients as well as to me.

In the ensuing months and years, I began to research issues related to attachment and loss as they pertain to identity formation. Dr. Margaret Mahler's theories on childhood development, called separation and individuation, became the basis for a therapeutic model I developed to help people survive, grow, and eventually thrive as adults post-divorce—a therapy spelled out in these pages that, with your work and commitment, can help you too. In my many years of clinical experience, I have become more and more convinced of the validity of understanding failed marriages from a developmental point of view. It's why I wrote this book.

For some—perhaps you—it may seem strange to view divorce as a new developmental phase in life. After all, by the time most people get divorced they're well into adulthood, so isn't their development as an individual complete? But consider that most marriages form when we are young. If done in an unhealthy, enmeshed way—in other words, by looking to the relationship to "fix" your problems as an individual— merging with another person in marriage, just as in childhood, can result in unclear personal boundaries, the inability to own and express who you are, underdeveloped self-esteem, and a struggle to take care of your individual needs.

In fact, we commonly look to our partners in marriage to make up for the attributes we lack. This interdependent situation doesn't discriminate toward any one gender, age, race, or social stratum. Instead, it's based on deficits established in the early developmental connections between child and parent, that crucial time when a parent should be supporting her child so she can become a strong, independent person. Just like in childhood, finding your place in the world as you move away from a primary relationship in adulthood is not an easy thing. Unconscious, often destructive coping mechanisms can take over, mechanisms that were established during the bonding period with your mother and father.

For me, that was definitely true—and being a twin complicated the picture even further. After a decade and a half of marriage and a lifetime as a twin, my identity as an individual had been murkier than I'd realized. The problematic interdependency of my marital relationship had allowed me to control, blame, and manipulate in destructive ways even I, as a therapist, had not seen. Looking to my patients, I saw the same patterns. But I also saw that these developmental deficits could be overcome, and that therapeutic work could in fact lead to a life post-divorce that was far more rewarding than people imagined.

* * *

Soon I began focusing my practice full-time on helping patients post-divorce. What had become clear to me was that there are two different processes people go through during this emotional roller-coaster ride. First, there is the grief of losing a loved one. No matter how bitter your marriage may have been, ghosts of the relationship haunt you, and you need to mourn the loss of both a partner and a partnership. Many people turn away from this period of mourning with the hope of just moving on. But as difficult as it can be, expressing grief, in your own individual way, is a necessity in the transition from marriage to singledom— and beyond to new relationships.

"After divorce, perhaps for the first time in your adult life, you must learn to develop a truly independent Self."

The second process I identified was the struggle for a more complete sense of personal identity. After divorce, perhaps for the first time in your adult life, you must learn to develop a truly independent Self. Like many people, you may never have had to face this situation. Since early adulthood, you've defined yourself in a collective sense. Post-divorce, you think, *If I'm not a part of a couple, than who am I? How am I going to do this on my own?* Personal values and goals that you may never have questioned before all of a sudden become subject to internal debate. Choices that another person once made with you or for you are now yours to decide alone. So to a great extent, divorce means learning to let go of the entity that was your partnership and finding a new path as the entity that is You.

I won't pretend that finding that path is easy. Navigating through the difficulties of the post-divorce period may be one of the most challenging times of your life—not unlike your adolescent years when you struggled to find yourself, or even those toddler years when you first learned to walk away from your parents and explore the world on your own. As in earlier phases of life, the journey after a divorce requires the courage to depart from what is safe and familiar, to establish your Self as opposed to who you were as part of a marital couple.

But the reward of this difficult journey is that transition means transformation, the development of personal power, renewed self-esteem, and the necessary prerequisites for successful future partnerships. If you understand the principles of developing your independent Self spelled out in this book and put them into practice, there is nothing that can keep you from a healthy, enriching relationship and life.

* * *

So where do we get started?

First, we'll take a look at the big picture. Everyone begins marriage with the intention of creating a healthy lifelong relationship. But again and again, marriages fail. To explore why, Chapter 1 will investigate the statistics of divorce and the many theories about where things go wrong. We'll also take a look at second and third divorces to get a clearer picture of why history often repeats itself.

In Chapter 2, we'll take a close look at grief and why it is so important to post-divorce healing. Many people define grief using Elisabeth Kübler-Ross's "five stages" model: Denial, Anger, Bargaining, Depression, and Acceptance. But does everyone experience loss in this way? Understanding that not all grief is created equal will give us a better picture of this necessary healing tool.

Chapter 3 will take a look at identity formation in child-hood. Understanding this developmental phase is crucial, since developing a new identity as a non-partnered person builds upon and mirrors identity formation in infancy and childhood. Following grief, establishing a stronger, more independent Self is the second step in healing from divorce, and the primary focus of this book. In this chapter we'll explore Dr. Margaret Mahler's theories of separation and individuation and see, through examples, how those developmental phases can play out in adulthood.

Not only do we experience development as individuals; couples go through developmental phases that follow Mahler's separation-individuation model too. And if a child's development was hindered at a certain phase, his or her development as part of a couple may follow the same path. Chapter 4 will explore those parallels, describing the various dynamics and intimacy issues that exist between two people who have entered a marriage with unresolved issues. Through exercises and examples, Chapter 5 will help you explore where your development may have been stunted—both when you were a child and as part of a couple—so that you may address those areas where you need to establish a stronger Self.

Next, in Chapter 6, we'll explore the steps you can take to move toward change. The exercises in this chapter will help you understand the defense mechanisms you developed in childhood and how they were carried into your adult relationships, particularly your marriage. Next, I will offer tools and techniques for developing a more successful and healthy interaction style, thereby avoiding the traps of enmeshment you experienced in the past or are currently facing.

Looking ahead to how fully developed Selves interact in a healthy relationship, a discussion of healthy boundaries and the three components of a good relationship will follow in Chapter 7, including the importance of self-awareness, mutual acceptance, and empathy. Individual counseling is often a part of the journey for people striving to complete their development and form healthy attachments to others as adults, so in Chapter 8 we'll explore the benefits from therapy, what to look for in a counselor, the time frame you can expect, and what the process involves.

* * *

Divorce is not a journey many people willingly take. It gives you a choice: to look honestly at yourself and your life—in ways you may never have before—and become richer for it, or to remain forever entangled in feeling you were wronged—though you very well may have been. Whether divorce is simply a life event to be endured or an exhilarating opportunity for change is determined by each individual's attitude toward it and his or her willingness to actively participate in their own growth. If you choose to learn from that introspection, you can experience something truly remarkable.

"The reward of this difficult journey is that transition means transformation, the development of personal power, renewed self-esteem, and the necessary prerequisites for successful future partnerships."

The book you hold in your hands will help you on that journey. It is unique in that it uses a developmental approach to help those struggling with the post-divorce landscape investigate root causes of the failure of their marriage, address those causes, and learn how to move forward to a stronger Self and more healthy, self-aware, and fulfilling relationships. Despite all the suffering and pain resulting from the breakdown of a marriage, there can be optimism and joy in the process too. Early childhood wounds that are carried into adulthood and lead to divorce can be healed.

But it takes time and work. So let's get started.

Chapter 1

Why Marriages Fail

Divorce, for most people, is not a decision made lightly. In fact, you may have spent months or years considering divorce, and agonized over the decision—a decision you thought you'd never be facing. Looking back to your courtship, wedding day, or the early part of your marriage, it might seem impossible that being divorced and single are in your future. Or, you might be incredulous that you ever felt this marriage could work in the first place. Yet no matter how you feel now, everyone begins marriage with the best of intentions. The day you decide that separation is the only answer to the problems in your relationship is never a happy one.

Still, it's a day many people face. In 2009, more than 1 million American couples got divorced. For first marriages, that amounts to 41 percent of all heterosexual unions—but the figures climb dramatically for succeeding marriages. Sixty percent of second marriages fail, and a shocking 73 percent of third marriages don't make it. Although the odds for marriage lasting might be great at a roulette table, they point to some serious problems when it comes to the health of marital relationships.

Depending on where you live, how much you earn, what your race is, how old you are, or whether or not your parents split up, divorce figures vary. People from Iowa tend to stay married in greater numbers than people from Arkansas. Caucasian and African American couples have higher rates of divorce than Asian and Hispanic Americans. Couples who marry later in life and maintain a higher level of income stay together more often than young people in lower income brackets. And if your parents divorced, your chances of a "till-death-do-us-part" marriage plummet dramatically.

Explaining the reasons behind all of this is difficult, even for the experts. There's no simple equation that tells us why divorce rates are higher in the Bible Belt than in the more liberal Northwest, or if New England, which has the lowest divorce rates, fosters marital stability because of racial or socioeconomic factors, religious demographics or a more communal culture. Many factors are involved. The complexity of the situation, however, doesn't prevent experts from studying divorce to try to discover the primary reasons marriages break down.

"It's unrealistic to expect that another person can complete you and make up for all the deficiencies of your upbringing, socialization, or personal development, but many people do."

Why People Divorce

Counselors, social workers, members of the clergy, sociologists, attorneys, journalists, and researchers have written widely on why marriages fail. Anyone exploring or experiencing divorce quickly discovers it's a complicated subject. But generally, the causes for divorce cited by professionals fall into two main categories: outside factors such as money, family, children, and work, and behavioral issues such as poor communication, infidelity, constant fighting, or physical abuse.

When my clients come to me either considering divorce, in the thick of a legal separation, or as newly single people, they usually have a fairly clear rationale for what went wrong in their marriage. Here are the top reasons I commonly encounter, in my practice as well as in the literature.

Unrealistic Expectations

Even the most well-meaning people enter into marriage with the belief that love will conquer all. As much as American culture promotes that idea—in movies, books, on television, and in magazines—falling in love and getting married are not the end of the story. It's unrealistic to expect that another person can complete you and make up for all the deficiencies of your upbringing, socialization, or personal development, but many people do. After all, it's what we're taught, from the first fairy tale our parents read to us to the teen magazines we flip through at the beach and the romantic comedies we watch as adults.

Women more than men seem to stumble with unrealistic expectations and focus on the "happily ever after" aspect of marriage more than the marriage itself. The enormous wedding industry feeds this romantic fantasy. In her book *The Starter Marriage and the Future of Matrimony*, Pamela Paul interviewed one woman whose expectations of matrimony didn't take into account the difficulties that arise after the honeymoon phase. The interviewee, whom Paul calls Isabel, "expected her marriage to be 'a nice life with nice things,' but mostly she devoted her attention to the wedding. During the engagement period, whenever she and her fiancé fought, which was often, Isabel wrote it off as prewedding jitters, assuming that once they were married, things would change." After the marriage, the fighting continued. At its core were two underdeveloped individuals with false expectations and poor coping mechanisms. Within a year, the couple was divorced.

Getting Married Young

The idea of a "starter marriage"—a union between people in their twenties that lasts less than five years and produces no children—points to another risk factor for divorce: getting married young. Couples under the age of twenty-five are statistically more prone to divorce than older couples. Since younger people tend to lack emotional maturity, earn less money, have fewer years of education, and/or marry because of an unplanned pregnancy, there can be a number of stressors in the relationship. "The higher the education level, higher the occupational level, higher the income, the less likely you are to divorce," says William V. D'Antonio, a sociologist at the Catholic University of America, in a *New York Times* article on divorce demographics. "Kids who drop out of high school and get married very quickly suffer from the strains of not being emotionally mature and not having the income to help weather the difficulties of marriage."

Peer pressure may also play a role. The same woman quoted above in Paul's book notes, "It's like this snowball effect. Once one person gets engaged, everybody has to get engaged. And then you get wrapped up in whose ring is bigger and who's getting married where and how much everything costs."

Clearly there are different economic dynamics going on in the teenage marriage and the marriage between college-educated couples with enough money for large weddings and expensive rings. But the goal is the same. As Isabel says, "You're expected to get married, buy a house, have two kids. I think everyone gets caught up in that, and I definitely did."

Poor Communication

Poor communication can take many forms: expecting a partner to read your mind, sharing private information outside the marriage, lying or omitting essential facts, fighting instead of discussing things in a rational way, or simply not talking enough.

Outside of deception, one of the biggest communication problems between partners is the false assumption that two people in a relationship see the world in the same way, value the same things, and express themselves similarly. We tend to forget that there are fundamental differences between all individuals, no matter how close their relationships. Steve Diehl, a pastor who provides marital counseling, describes a couple who continually ran up against this problem, even when they were trying to show that they cared for one another. For example, when the husband cleaned the house, the wife perceived his work as an expression of criticism, not love, and when the wife arranged flowers for the bedroom as a caring gesture, the husband hardly noticed, thinking she was doing it for herself. "They each expressed love to the other in the way they wanted to receive it ... Love is not best expressed by what you like to do, but rather by what the other person likes you to do. To love in this way, you must learn the other spouse's 'language,'" says Diehl.

These examples may pale in comparison with the red-button issues in your former marriage, but they illustrate how easy it can be to make assumptions about others' thoughts and actions, forgetting that the two of you are separate individuals with personal histories and viewpoints very different from one another's.

Strictly Defined Gender Roles

As the last example shows, gender can play a big part in our expectations, the way we communicate, the things we value, the way we interpret others' actions, and the things we overlook. Men and women see the world in different ways, and it can be hard to understand when your partner doesn't have the same viewpoint as you. It can be just as difficult, however, when your spouse expects you to conform to strictly defined gender roles—for example, a relationship in which the male is very assertive and the female a submissive helpmate. If people are assigned roles they aren't comfortable with based on models from childhood or other, external sources, they limit themselves as individuals. This can cause conflict—both for the couple and for the individual unwillingly subscribing to his or her role.

I see the expectation that men and women should adhere to strictly defined gender roles often, in my practice as well as in articles from couples counselors, particularly religious professionals. It can be an especially difficult point for individuals whose upbringing and religion taught them that this is the way they should behave. And those gender roles extend to all sorts of other sticking points, including money management, the division of work in the home, questions of childrearing, and sex.

"If your parents divorced, your own marriage is much more likely to end in divorce too. Behavioral influences that caused divorce in your primary family are handed down to you."

Poor Money Management

The subject of money and how to manage it has the capacity to trigger powerful subjective emotions. That's because the way individuals think about money is tied to their unique family history, with all the conflicts, needs, fears, and desires money represented in their families when they were children. For that reason, money is chockfull of psychological, emotional, and symbolic meanings. It's no wonder it's often named as the main source of conflict in a marriage.

Some of the ways people's relationships with money play themselves out are equating money with love; buying things to soothe feelings of inadequacy or low self-worth; spending during times of depression, anger, boredom, or as an act of retaliation; or equating money with caretaking and security. During a marriage as well as a divorce, all of these associations can be challenged, causing a lot of emotional turmoil.

Having Parents Who Divorced

The statistics are pretty clear that if your parents divorced, your own marriage is much more likely to end in divorce too. Behavioral influences that caused divorce in your primary family are handed down to you, just as associations with money are.

According to PsychPage's "Relationship Reasons for Divorce," among adult children of divorced parents, 60 percent marry and 40 percent of them eventually divorce. In contrast, among adult children from intact families, 80 percent marry and 9 percent divorce. Behavioral influences drive the figures. Personal problems, self-reported as people who are easily angered, hurt, or made jealous, those who show poor money-management skills, and those who have an affair, "were twice as likely in marriages in which both partners' parents had divorced compared to marriages in which neither partner's parents had divorced." These issues tended to show up early, too—in the first four years of the marriage.

Infidelity and Lack of Intimacy

As reported by couples therapists, as many as 50 percent of divorces occur because of cheating. Infidelity can mean a sexual relationship outside the marriage or an emotional one—or a combination of the two. Men are more likely than women to cheat sexually, while it's more common that women will cheat emotionally. Internet affairs fall into the second category.

Although an affair may be the rationale given for a divorce, lack of intimacy is often the more succinct reason. "Most people do not have affairs because they want to hurt their partners," reports Richard Niolon. "Rather, they feel lonely, or distant, or desperate for love, and these powerful feelings can make an affair very tempting, and the chance to meet these powerful emotional needs overpowering." Cheating may also occur when couples see their marriage as otherwise a good one—in fact, 34 percent of women and 56 percent of men having affairs report being happy in their marriage.

But the revelation of infidelity is nonetheless devastating, causing depression, guilt, shame, intense sadness, and rage. The trauma of betrayal is often so great that it is very difficult to overcome.

* * *

There are many other reasons people cite for why they sought divorce: mental and physical abuse, lack of compatibility, addiction, conflict over children, work problems, and personality conflicts, to name a few. Interestingly, there are definite milestones within marriages when these sources of conflict become unendurable: couples tend to divorce within five to seven years of the wedding when they can't resolve high-conflict issues, and the ten- to twelve-year anniversary mark is when people most often split because of loss of intimacy and connection.

There is also a set time frame when people remarry after a divorce: on average, within two and a half years.

Divorcing the Second or Third Time Around

The high rate of remarriage illustrates our universal need to bond—and to do so legally, in marriage. In fact, 2010 statistics show that 75 percent of divorced men and women in the United States remarry. People are obviously optimistic that they have learned from the problems that contributed to their first divorce.

The high divorce rates in second and third marriages, however, suggest otherwise. Though it might seem that after going through the difficulties of marriage and divorce once we'd be better equipped to forge happy, healthy relationships the second or third time around, the statistics tell a different story.

One of the reasons is comfort level. "Once a person discovers that he or she can manage a divorce, they are less scared of going through the process again," reports therapist Jay Granat. Another reason is that individuals and couples follow the same strategy for problem resolution in second and third marriages as they did in their first one. And, not surprisingly, the problems they are trying to resolve are often the same too.

There's good reason for this; in fact, it is the basis for most divorces and the focus of this book: *we bring our underdeveloped identities and unsuccessful coping behaviors from past relationships, whether they're romantic or familial ties, into our new relationships.* If conflict over money was a problem in a first marriage— or in the primary family—it's likely to be a problem in the second marriage too. The same is true for infidelity, gender role issues, poor communication, unrealistic expectations, and all the other reasons cited for divorce. These causes do not arise independent of everything that came before them. They come from how we learned to act and interact earlier in life.

"Each person bears the full responsibility for determining how they will meet the realities of their life from today on. Becoming mindful of that is an important part of the healing process."

For that reason, conflict tends to come to a head fairly early for people married more than once. Twenty-five percent of second or third marriages end in the first five years. So clearly, although people have a strong desire to connect with another person and repartner, they are not doing a better job of it.

* * *

In many cases, couples can identify strategies to deal with the internal and external conflicts in their marriage. Taking a money management class, breaking off an affair, or committing to improved communication, for example, can certainly help to improve the relationship and resolve some of the issues so often cited for divorce. But as professor of sociology Paul Amato states, "Personal problems do not appear to be short-term reactions to a deteriorating marriage"—instead, they are behavioral responses attempting to manage more fundamental conflicts, and therefore addressing them, though helpful, does not address the core problem at hand. The spending or the cheating or the silent treatment, the arguing or the withholding of sex or the eighty-hour work weeks are actually outward expressions of something much more deep-seated.

Years of reflecting on the true nature of the marital bond, in my personal experience with marriage and divorce as well as through my ensuing clinical work and research, has convinced me that the core problem of failed marriages lies in the tendency of partners to look to each other, rather than to themselves, to heal their inner pain from childhood and create happiness. When we relinquish ownership of our own deficits and project onto our partners idealized and unrealistic expectations, we shift the responsibility for our personal development onto the wrong source.

Living together on a daily basis chisels away at these idealized projections, leaving the disappointed and angry spouse feeling that his or her partner is not the person they married. In reality, they never were. From there, marital problems unfold, sometimes subtly and sometimes not, as we will see in Chapter 4. In too many cases, these problems lead to divorce.

"No marriage can succeed until the two people in it are able to see and express themselves as full individuals. That is when real transformation in the relationship can take place."

During marriage or in its aftermath, it's necessary to stop relying on those idealizations and expectations, and in their place take full responsibility for personal well-being. Consider the difference between the following: Instead of accusing your partner with "You're making me angry," you say to yourself, "I feel angry. Where in me is that coming from?" You have to acknowledge that using a spouse—or any other outside factor—to prop up the shaky hold you have on your sense of Self simply doesn't work. In order to heal from the divorce, the emphasis has to shift to personal growth.

At the heart of the matter is this: No marriage can succeed until the two people in it are able to see and express themselves as full individuals. That's when real transformation in the relationship can take place. In fact, my clinical work has shown me that marital crises, particularly crises that end in divorce, are the *direct* result of two underdeveloped, immature adults attempting to create a successful and mature partnership. It's simply not possible for two flawed individuals to create a healthy marriage. A relationship is only as good as the individuals in it.

To some degree, we are all underdeveloped as individuals. That's because as imperfect human beings—none of us is perfect—parents fall short of helping their children develop complete inner selves, a discussion we'll explore in Chapter 3. So does this mean a divorce rate of 50 percent is inevitable? No! But reversing the trend requires a dramatic change in the way we view ourselves and our partnerships. Developing strong personal identities, both prior to and during marriage, is the way to honoring ourselves and our relationships.

Many people passively accept marital failure because the alternative requires an entirely different approach—and that's not easy. After divorce, most of us are inclined to ignore the call to reinvention because we fear letting go of our old Selves (our egos have a great deal of difficulty letting go of anything!). For many, divorce is a terrifying experience; we're desperate to know that things will work out, yet all we can see is the abyss.

The fear we may experience in leaving behind our spouses and becoming independent can't be overemphasized. It's frightening because the journey requires letting go of some of the fundamentals of who we have been and what we believed about ourselves.

But we can't expect our partners, past, present, or future, to take the responsibility of living out all the aspects of our lives if we can't live them out for ourselves. A quote that captures the process perfectly is this: "The paradox of individuation"—that is, becoming your own person—"is that we best serve the interests of [a] relationship by becoming sufficiently developed in ourselves that we don't feed off another person." It's only when we can be happy on our own that we have the best chance of success in marriage. Paradoxically, it's only when we no longer *need* a partner that we are most likely to find one who best complements us, supports us, and makes life more full.

For the marriage we have lost, that chance is gone, and that loss must be grieved. But the loss is also an opportunity—to look deeply at ourselves and make a decision about how we interact in relationships going forward. Each person bears the full responsibility for determining how they will meet the realities of their life from today on. Becoming mindful of that is an important part of the healing process.

But first we must face the grief of losing a partner, a relationship, the future we planned for, and our identity as a coupled person. In the next chapter, we will take a look at this grieving process, from its beginning to its end.

Exercise for Chapter 1:

1. Describe, in a short paragraph, the main reason, as you see it, why your marriage failed.

2. Do you see this failure as mainly one person's fault? If so, whose?

3. If you see your partner as the main person at fault, what were his or her contributing behaviors? If you take blame for the end of your marriage, what were your contributing behaviors?

4. In either case, did similar behaviors exist in your or your spouse's primary family?

5. How did your parents deal with similar situations? How did your spouse's?

6. If you were to begin a new relationship and saw warning signs of trouble, how would you handle things differently than you did in your current marriage?

Chapter 2

The Importance of Grief to Post-Divorce Healing

From the time we are born, we attach—to our parents, our extended family, our friends, our surroundings, and our things. We attach, and we accumulate. And where there is attachment, inevitably there will be loss. Yet, to our own misfortune, we don't learn to let go in the same way we learn to acquire. Instead, when loss happens—through death, divorce, or disaster—it takes us off guard, and we don't know how to deal with it. Our natural inclination is "I don't want to have to feel this pain, so how do I get out of it?"

That was just my reaction when I went through my own divorce. After my husband left, I understood for the first time how someone could actually die of a broken heart. I had no concept of how to deal with loss. I was only marginally helped to understand the upheaval of emotions that I was experiencing. Nobody told me that dealing with my grief was part of the healing process, that it was okay to feel untethered, and that I actually *needed* to go through that difficult time. As grief specialist George Bonanno writes, it's a surprising fact that despite the ubiquity of loss—almost all of us will experience it at some point in life, and commonly more than once—most people know next to nothing about what to expect and how to handle the emotional turbulence when it happens to them.

"Despite the ubiquity of loss, most people know next to nothing about what to expect and how to handle the emotional turbulence when it happens to them."

What Is Grief?

From the outside grief may appear to be a one-dimensional emotion, synonymous with sadness. But in reality, grief is very complex. It consists of a mixture of all of the raw feelings you have in response to loss, not exclusively sorrow. These feelings, both positive and negative, sometimes contradictory, can include longing, fear, anger, love, hate, regret, guilt, and deprivation. The closer you were to your spouse, the greater the feelings of imbalance you may experience. Russell Friedman and John James offer a definition that embraces the complexity, as well as the universality of this multifaceted emotional state: "Grief is the normal and natural reaction to loss of any kind. It is the entire range of naturally occurring human emotions that accompany loss."

Whether you are the leaver or the left, divorce plunges you into these turbulent waters. Once there, there are no hard and fast rules about how you'll move through the grieving process. This is in contrast to what most people expect. They anticipate following psychiatrist Elizabeth Kübler-Ross's five stages of grief: Denial ("This can't be happening to me." "I can't actually be doing this."), Anger ("It isn't fair. What did I do to deserve this?"), Bargaining ("How do I get him/her back?" "Maybe I should stick this out and try to make it work."), Depression ("I feel hopeless." "Nothing matters anymore."), and Acceptance ("This relationship is over." "I will be okay now."). Though for many years specialists subscribed to this model, today grief is more commonly perceived as less linear and more individualized. Robert A. Neimeyer, editor of *Meaning Reconstruction and the Experience of Loss*, says, "Highly individual processes of meaning making are at the heart of grief dynamics"—in other words, we each express grief in a very personal way.

Although each individual will experience loss according to his or her own unique circumstances, there are some fairly universal reactions. Most people in the midst of grief experience:

- A sense of numbness
- Difficulty sleeping
- Loss of appetite
- Inability to concentrate
- Feeling negative
- Lack of energy
- Low self-esteem/feelings of failure

Generally, at its beginning—and sometimes for extended periods of time—grief brings about the need to turn away from the demands of day-to-day life, so it's not surprising that feeling numb, almost anesthetized, is the most common initial psychological response to loss. As Bonanno states in his book *The Other Side of Sadness*, when we're grieving "there seems to be less need to pay attention to the world around us, so we are able to put aside normal, everyday concerns and turn our attention inwards." The rush of physiological as well as psychological discomfort cues us to the fact that we need to take notice of and care for ourselves, in body as well as in spirit.

Male and Female Expressions of Grief

Though men and women's physiological and psychological responses to loss may be similar, the way the two genders express their grief outwardly is often very different. Men are expected to be strong, and so they tend to show little emotion and are very self-protective. Women, on the other hand, are usually more freely emotional. Women typically find comfort in connection and talking about their emotions, while men are more likely to be quiet, withdrawn, and somewhat isolated. Men may even consciously distract themselves or try to forget anything that reminds them of their loss. If men's emotions do begin to break through, they often attempt to gain even greater control over their feelings so it doesn't happen again. Keep in mind that whether the expression of your grief is more reflective of the male or female model, the goal should be the same: growth from the experience and a healthy reengagement in life.

Cultural Expectations of Grief

Anyone who's experienced grief or tried to comfort someone else who's in the midst of loss is sure to have heard or said these familiar phrases: "Time heals all wounds." "Keep busy." "Just move on." As well-intentioned as this advice may be, the idea that grief can be compartmentalized, overridden, or forgotten simply doesn't reflect the way we experience loss.

The idea that time will resolve grief is probably the greatest misconception. There's a mistaken idea that after enough time passes something will magically change to make us feel whole again. If only it were so easy. In truth, time itself doesn't heal; it's what you do within time that will help you complete the pain caused by the loss.

Distraction, like time, doesn't help you experience grief in order to complete it—and that's the goal for recovery. Keeping busy to avoid addressing your pain simply moves that work farther down the road, where eventually you'll need to face it. The same is true for blocking out the pain and "moving on"— or attempting to hand your recovery work off to someone waiting expectantly on the sidelines.

"There is a mistaken idea that after enough time passes something will magically change to make us feel whole again."

Take, for example, Bob,* a patient of mine. He was on the verge of trying to bypass his grief when he came to me in distress and confusion over his recent divorce. When his wife left, shouldering him with the family business and two small children, he, like so many people, was looking for a way to avoid the pain of dealing with loss. In his case, a woman he'd met online almost immediately after the divorce decree was signed offered a solution. She promised to step in to help out not only with the business but also with the kids. For Bob the proposition was extremely

---

*Names and details throughout the book have been changed to protect patient confidentiality.

tempting (who wouldn't want to take that offer?), and he was seriously considering it. But deep down, he knew this shortcut to getting over his failed marriage and "moving on" was too good to be true—and so he called me. As we started our work, Bob agreed that he would not make any major decisions during therapy. Only with that stipulation in place could we begin to establish the individuation he so desperately needed.

Self-Examine, Not "Other-Examine"

In addition to looking for an escape route from pain, another natural human tendency when it comes to divorce is to blame the other party and place yourself in the role of victim. But as Friedman and James say, "We need to self-examine, not other-examine." As long as you feel that someone else is solely responsible for your loss, you won't be able to recover by developing your Self beyond the complicated dynamics and dysfunctions of your former marriage.

I fell into this trap during my divorce. I used to say to myself that if my ex-husband would just call me and say, "I'm sorry for what I did," everything would be all right. My role as the victim would be validated, and so would his role as the villain. But in truth, it wasn't so simple. Like so many people going through divorce, my sense of rightness or self-righteousness kept me from being totally honest with myself. As much as my husband deserved blame for the breakup of our marriage, there were two people involved in our union, and I needed to examine my own actions in the marriage in order to accept my part of the responsibility. It was only through this work that I could heal and move forward.

The Power of Human Resilience

Looking back, what I marvel at now is how resilient I actually was, despite all the anger and sadness that sometimes overwhelmed me. Although it can be hard to realize when you're in the midst of grief, people generally are resilient—much more so than they realize. That's not to say that people are not deeply wounded by the loss of their marriage—there's no question the pain of divorce runs deep—but somehow they manage to regain their equilibrium, despite the hurt.

What's interesting is that we have this false notion that grief is a constant, unbroken state. But even in the short term, when our pain is at its greatest, grief is interspersed with moments of happiness, even joy and laughter—that complexity of emotion I talked about earlier. If you've ever experienced the death of a loved one, you can probably remember times when you were able to smile about the memories of the person who died, or share a funny story with others who were grieving alongside you—even in your darkest moments. Divorce is like that too. Except for in those minority cases where there is an underlying pathology present, the human mind seeks a path to recovery. I believe people grieve in so many different ways because of our resilience and our capacity for healing. In fact, it is fair and right that people can expect to recover, no matter how great their loss.

Signs of Incomplete Grieving

Grief, dramatic and even traumatic as it may be, is a process and a normal, healthy reaction to a loss. But grief can be inhibited when the natural flow of feelings about the loss is shut off through attempts to deny, delay, or displace difficult emotions. The result is unhealthy or unsuccessful grief.

"A natural human tendency when it comes to divorce is blaming the other party and placing yourself in the role of victim."

Since most of us have so little experience with loss, it helps to know the major pitfalls and avoidance techniques that are used to circumvent the grieving process. The following are some of the places many people experiencing loss lose their way on the road to recovery:

Avoiding grief or seeing it with fear. Every person experiencing loss needs to make a conscious decision to choose recovery and completion over avoidance, isolation, and fear. As Friedman and James put it, "Grief means claiming your circumstances instead of your circumstances claiming you and your happiness." That's hard, because loss is never easy, particularly when it encompasses not just the loss of your spouse but of all of the hopes, dreams, and expectations you had for your future together. It's a frightening situation to face, and one that can take a long time to get over. Even after you begin to recover, there will be times when you feel sad or scared and want to talk about it. You should expect that, and not feel that you are losing ground when those emotions strike. Grief is a wound that needs attention in order to heal, and it takes courage to face the pain.

My patient Susan showed just this sort of courage when particularly difficult emotions surfaced following her divorce. Prior to that time, Susan prided herself as a confident, independent, and adventurous woman. She loved to travel and engage in new experiences. But with the breakup of her marriage, her outgoing nature dissolved. She was overwhelmed with anxiety, to the point of becoming agoraphobic, and stopped venturing more than a few miles from home. As we explored her fears, it became apparent that her adventurous spirit depended on the active attachment to her husband, without whom her independence was shaky. Though a period of isolation and reflection is a normal part of grief, Susan's anxiety and fearfulness weren't allowing her to reengage with the world, and this overwhelming fear was the sign of uncompleted grief. After several months of therapy, including work on establishing Susan as a strong, capable individual, her adventurous nature began to return, and eventually she started planning a cross-country trip to visit a college friend.

Idealizing or demonizing the people associated with grief. We all have a tendency to look back at phases in our lives as either the best or the worst of times, but life is never that black and white. Good times are always mixed with challenging moments, and vice versa. Although it can be tempting to rewrite the past in either a rosy or dark light, revisionist history won't help you complete the pain caused by your loss. As much as possible, you need to look on the past with an objective eye and acknowledge the truth of your relationship in order to help you complete your loss.

It's common to demonize ex-spouses following divorce, but I've also encountered idealized versions of failed marriages. That happened with Sara, a client who sought my help after her husband declared their marriage over. In our early conversations, Sara embellished their life together to such a degree that I was confused about why it had ended. Sara repeatedly described Sam, her ex-husband, in saintlike terms, unwilling to place any blame on him for walking out. Instead, she shouldered the full burden of the divorce, telling me, "I didn't communicate well. I yelled. I was impatient with him. I liked to micromanage him. I ruined a perfectly good marriage." Only after numerous sessions did she finally admit that Sam's passivity and laziness irritated and annoyed her, often filling her with outrage. Idealizing Sam in the early stages of her treatment and taking the full blame for the divorce enabled Sara to deny uncomfortable feelings, like resentment over Sam's childlike dependency needs.

More often, patients complain bitterly about their ex-spouses. I cannot help but think of Janet who earned millions of dollars on Wall Street and does not let a session go by when she is not voicing outrage about the alimony the court awarded her former husband. There is a strong tendency to get obsessed with the idea that our former spouse harmed us, and while many times they have, clarity of vision is necessary. Consider the things you wish you had said or done differently in the marriage alongside those things your spouse said or did that were hurtful. Although expressing anger can be satisfying in the moment, and is often a healthy way to deal with loss if balanced with other coping skills, it can also become a defense mechanism that separates you from independence. Sustained anger keeps you from being totally honest about the whole experience of your marital relationship and, most importantly, can prevent you from focusing on building your identity apart from your spouse.

Experiencing symptoms typical of depression. If prolonged, the same symptoms that signal grief—numbness, difficulty sleeping, loss of appetite, lack of optimism, low self-esteem, lack of sexual interest—are signs that the griever is not addressing his or her loss as they should. Because depression and grief manifest themselves in similar ways, it's important to be able to distinguish between the two. If the symptoms of grief persist for a year or more, clinical depression may be setting in, and that is a separate situation from grief. There is circumstantial depression, which is a part of the grieving process, and clinical depression, which is a medical condition. Monitor your feelings carefully with the help of a professional if you feel clinical depression is taking over.

Experiencing psychosomatic, or physical, symptoms. As a part of circumstantial or even clinical depression, grief sometimes expresses itself as physical illness. It's not unusual for people in the midst of loss to experience headaches, stomach aches, and anxiety. My patients often tell me, "One minute I think I'm fine, and the next I'm throwing up." When these physical symptoms persist, they are acting as a substitute for unresolved sorrow and signal that additional, professional help is needed.

Masking grief with destructive behaviors. It's very common for people to turn to unhealthy behaviors as a way of anesthetizing themselves to the pain of loss. Common coping mechanisms include drinking, doing drugs, engaging in sex with multiple partners, working constantly, shopping excessively, and gambling. In some cases, these coping mechanisms existed prior to the divorce, and may have even contributed to the breakup of the marriage. Whether that's true or not for you, all of these behaviors serve as a means of avoidance, and all can eventually compound the problems associated with loss. Until you remove the obstacles that will prevent you from exploring and embracing yourself as an individual, you won't take responsibility for personal well-being in order to recover.

"Every person experiencing loss needs to make a conscious decision to choose recovery and completion over isolation and avoidance."

The Consequences of Not Dealing with Grief

Whether conscious or unconscious, not dealing with grief can have a lifelong negative impact on a person's capacity for happiness. By not grieving, whether that means masking your grief with destructive behaviors or doing your best to bury those difficult feelings, you limit your ability to trust and be open and loving in another relationship. People who choose not to grieve often choose fear in its place, becoming overly self-protective and hypervigilant in their approach to future relationships.

"Playing it safe" has consequences beyond living life in fear. If you don't examine your failed relationship and address who you are as an individual outside of a partnership, history can repeat itself. The astronomical divorce rate for second and third marriages is a testament to that fact. Lack of self-examination results in people repeating the same mistakes they made in their first marriage, often with the same outcome.

When you choose not to engage in grief and letting go, you limit your life's possibilities. Why lock yourself in that jail cell when the key is within reach?

Steps to Recovery

There are steps you can take to begin the process of completing your grief and moving on. Remember, this is your journey, your choice to proactively move forward.

Make a choice to recover. The first step is to make a conscious choice to go through grief. You can't change what has happened, but you can decide how you will respond to it. Remember, you must claim your circumstances so they don't claim you.

Examine what you wish had been better/different. An awareness of your own contribution to the failed relationship is vital. Although we all want to find a scapegoat when life doesn't go as planned, taking on the role of victim is not productive. Instead, you have to look at your spouse and yourself as whole people, meaning you have to look at the positive as well as the negative. In the lifetime of experiences you've shared, what do you wish you had done differently in your marriage? What do you wish your spouse had done? Examining these details and forgiving yourself and your spouse for the shortcomings in your relationship will allow you to integrate a full and honest picture of the marriage in order to move on. If you don't see your marriage in an honest way—with all the ups and downs that were part of it—the accumulation of a life of unsaid and undone things will contribute to a sense of incompleteness.

Find new meaning in your life. Don't get stuck in the past and end up walking around with a terrible fear of being hurt again and a desire to protect yourself at all costs. It can be a self-fulfilling prophecy. Instead, look to the possibilities this life event brings. You may have always wanted to travel, explore your artistic side, move to a different city, parent your children in a different way—the possibilities are endless. In addition, you now have the opportunity to live out fuller, healthier relationships. As Friedman and James advise, "Those who are anxious about their relationships will engage in coercive and distrusting ways of dealing with conflict, which will bring about the very outcome they fear." Those coercive, distrusting ways can overshadow other aspects of your life too. If there is another option, don't you want to take it?

Realize that you can't undo the past, but you can find ways to deal with the emotions that accompany those memories. The goal is to complete your unfinished memories. That doesn't mean you will forget your loved one, but it does mean you can leave behind the hurt.

Mourn your loss. The grief you feel is not just for the loss of your spouse. There are many, many losses associated with divorce. Complete your relationship to the pain and disappointment that this person, this marriage, caused you. The mourning period is a time to heal and recover, to regain your equilibrium and capacity for living fully.

Forgive your former spouse. Forgiving is not condoning bad behavior; it's making a commitment to not hold on to the resentment that behavior cost you. It's making a conscious effort to say, "This resentment is harming me, I need to let it go." Forgiving does *not* mean approaching your former spouse to absolve him or her of the harm they caused you—people can forgive without ever talking to the other person again. Instead, it's a way of setting those emotions free, of saying, "I don't want to be burdened with this anymore. It happened. I have feelings about it, but I am going to release it so that I can move on with my life."

Seek individual or group counseling. More often than not, it's not enough to talk to your close friends when going through the trauma of divorce. People tend to see things through their own lenses and to have difficulty advising others on their own unique circumstances. An individual therapist who specializes in divorce counseling and/or a divorce support group can shepherd you through the transition. Whether you are consumed with pain, anger, guilt, or all three, a wise professional can help you turn a trauma into a turning point.

Take good care of yourself. It's very important to take care of your physical needs while you are experiencing grief. Eat well. Exercise. Seek out other people instead of retreating into solitude. Find empowerment in trying something new. Avoid those who are not investing in their own lives. Not long after my divorce, a friend asked me to participate in a marathon. I'd never run in my life, but I took the challenge, and my sense of accomplishment as I trained and met my goal of crossing the finish line was incredibly empowering.

Actively Completing Grief Takes Time

Love does not die quickly. Sometimes recovery will feel like an agonizingly slow process of two steps forward and one step back. Abigail Trafford, author of *Crazy Time: Surviving Divorce and Building a New Life*, estimates that it takes one year to recover for every five years of marriage. Although recovery time can vary depending on your makeup and history with loss, my experience says she is right on target. Your process is complete when you can release any pain you associated with your marriage, including the unrealistic expectation of getting something from your spouse that he or she was unable to give you.

Although it may be hard to imagine at this point, the reality is that no matter how devastated you are and no matter how long it takes, you can work through this and successfully move on. Getting through this time will be an exercise in reaching deep into yourself and finding survival strategies you may never have needed before. The key is to honor your grieving process. Don't try to short-circuit it.

Exercise for Chapter 2:

1. What do you wish you had done differently in your marriage?

2. What do you wish your spouse had done differently?

3. Write out the note of forgiveness you wish you could receive from your spouse.

4. Write out a note of forgiveness to your spouse, not saying what happened in your marriage was okay, but letting him or her know you are putting it behind you so you can move forward without the hurt.

5. List new three things you would like to try. Let your imagination run wild: Would you like to run a 5K, learn how to play the piano, take a pottery class, write a short story?

6. Set a goal for yourself to do one of those three things. Ask a friend to join you if you don't want to do it alone.

7. List those things you are currently doing that you would like to avoid. (Some examples might be drinking more than you should, not eating well, gambling or shopping too much.)

8. Choose one thing to work on improving.

9. List five people you enjoy spending time with.

10. Call one and set up a time for lunch or coffee.

Chapter 3

Childhood Identity Formation

There are a couple of things we know without a doubt: the divorce rate is frighteningly high, and that figure reflects the difficulty people have in sustaining long-term relationships. What people don't know, for the most part, is why.

To understand failed marriages better, we need to step back in time—not to when we met our spouse, or even our first romance, but to early childhood, when we were taught about human connection from a single, crucial relationship: the relationship we had with our primary caregiver, typically our mother.

What most people don't realize is that the problems they experience in their adult relationships are rooted in events that occurred when they were infants and children, when identity and selfhood were formed. During the critical developmental phase of birth to age three, 90 percent of the brain's adult size is realized, and the majority of the brain systems responsible for the way we behave, emote, interact, and function take shape. The socialization skills we acquire from our primary caregiver become a template for all the human bonds that follow; it's through this connection that we learn how to empathize, love, share, comfort, control aggression and frustration, and otherwise form healthy relationships.

This bonding period is an evolutionary necessity. Our brains are structured to connect to one another because we need human relationships in order to survive, in all the manifestations of that word. Our interaction with and attachment to others allow us to learn, work, form friendships, find mates, procreate, and raise children. Humans are social animals, so it's important that we learn how to interact in healthy ways from a very early age.

However, no bond between mother and child is perfect, just as no later relationship is. As any parent will tell you, it's impossible to interpret a child's needs fully and react to them perfectly every time. Fortunately children are resilient, and don't need perfect parental modeling to form a strong parent-child bond—and strong relationships later in life. If the attachment between mother and child is compromised for short periods of time, for example when the parent or child is tired, frustrated, angry, or sick, repair can take place soon thereafter.

But there are many cases where bonding is compromised on a longer-term basis. This can happen when the primary parent is absent because she is seriously ill, unable to be with the child because of work or schooling, poorly educated about the importance of early bonding to human development (as many people are) and therefore inattentive, or, in extreme cases, neglectful, abusive, or completely out of the picture. On the other end of the spectrum, healthy bonding can also be negatively affected by overly present parents who are also anxious, controlling, fearful, or manipulative.

To understand how these various scenarios play out in an adult's capacity to form successful relationships, we need to take a look at the developmental process from birth to age three.

For that, let's turn to Margaret Mahler, who discovered the process by which human beings are shaped.

"What most people don't realize is that the problems they experience in their adult relationships are rooted in events that occurred when they were infants and children, when identity and selfhood were formed."

Mahler's Model of Early Childhood Development

Mahler began her revolutionary work studying early childhood development in the late fifties at the Master's Children's Center in New York City. She created a research setting where she observed the natural interactions between mothers and their children twice a month for the first three years of the children's lives. From these observations, she developed her theories of separation-individuation, theories that describe childhood identity formation, or as she termed it, "psychological birth."

From the initial symbiotic bond the mother forms with her child on through the four subphases of the separation-individuation process, all of which we will explore in this chapter, the mother's role is absolutely critical to the child's psychological development. Mom becomes the measure by which the infant can successfully transition from being psychologically merged with her in its first month outside the womb to becoming a healthy and independent being by age three. A mother's unconditional love, in tandem with her acceptance of her child's

47

burgeoning identity, guides the child's growth. If that love and acceptance are missing or deficient, the child's psychological birth will be impeded. Ideally, during these early years child and parent experience a satisfying, mutually happy, and loving relationship.

To get a better sense of the progression from symbiosis to the separation-individuation stages of differentiation, practicing, rapprochement, and the consolidation of individuality, let's take a look at each, from both the child's and mother's point of view.

Symbiosis – During the first months of human life, an infant is focused almost completely on his or her internal needs and doesn't recognize that the external world exists separate from itself. It spends much of its time sleeping and growing, and when its needs arise—for food, warmth, or comfort—it cries out for gratification, although there is little awareness of what or who meets these needs. Because the newborn has no past, it has no psychology or sense of Self. To support this undifferentiated state, the physical unity of mother and newborn that existed during pregnancy needs to be re-created psychologically outside the womb. Mahler called this process "the second birth" and the initial connection between mother and child "symbiosis."

To form an impression of her baby, Mom must rely partly on the conscious and unconscious fantasies she had about her child while pregnant; the rest she draws from his or her real characteristics. In this way, the foundation for emotional attachment between the two is built.

As the weeks and months progress, the baby's exclusive internal focus on sensations gives way to an increased awareness of its environment. For example, a baby will stop feeding and smile when he hears his mother's voice. He'll look directly at Mom as she holds and talks to him. At five months, he'll gurgle and coo, sounds that are believed to be the beginning of human verbal communication.

Symbiosis is the foundation of the child's developing ability to relate to and empathize with others; these human faculties are learned as an extension of a healthy mother-child bond. If Mom is doing her job well and adequately nourishing and protecting her child, he will trustingly open his arms to reach out to the world.

During symbiosis, mother and infant mutually respond to each other in a blissful way. What is unique about the mother-infant interaction during the symbiotic phase is the intensity of the mother and baby's mutual pleasure and attunement to one another. Without this harmony, the child will be less prepared for the next phase of his development.

Differentiation – The differentiation subphase begins at about five months, when the outside world begins to come more under the baby's control. As his sense of Self develops, he starts to realize that his mouth, hands, and eyes can make things happen. By this time interactions between baby and mother such as bathing, rocking, and diapering have become comfortably ritualized. Despite this reassuring structure, Mom and baby are no longer as perfectly attuned as they once were. Although the infant continues to signal his needs to his mother, he is simultaneously developing an ability to see her as a separate person who may or may not gratify his needs exactly as he wants her

49

to. He is also becoming increasingly aware of people who are not Mom or other members of his family.

It's very important for the mother to develop a heightened ability to read her child's cues during differentiation. Babies at this stage are learning to interact, but it takes a while for them to do it successfully, and Mom must be patient. Since this is also a time when infants become more interested in the world around them, including relating to others, Mom must be comfortable letting go of the blissful symbiotic union she previously enjoyed with her child so he can maximize his developing capacity for exploration. Children at this age will often sit at their mother's feet, given comfort in the fact that Mom is nearby but also pleasure in discovering the world outside of her arms.

Practicing – At around ten months, the child begins a full-on exploration of his environment, what Mahler called "having a love affair with the world." He becomes more courageous, and his need to distance from his mother becomes even clearer and more pronounced. Although the infant uses Mom as a "home base," or anchor, he is ready to start exploring away from her, coming back when in need of comfort, to share discoveries, or to gratify some other need. Baby's developing mobility in the form of crawling and walking lets Mom know that he is outgrowing the old closeness they had. Practicing is a joyous time when the toddler's focus is almost exclusively on flexing his muscles and exploring the world around him.

During the practicing subphase, it is Mom's responsibility to encourage and facilitate her child's new and wondrous experiences. There needs to be a balance of respect for the child's emerging Self and the parental support that was established during the symbiotic phase. It's not uncommon for some mothers to interpret their child's necessary steps to becoming a separate person as a sign of rejection or an indication of the mother's own inadequacies. Misinterpreting a child's need to establish his sense of identity as a personal failure, which may be a sign of the mother's unresolved issues of autonomy, is a sure way to inhibit his development. As Madeline Levine says in *Teach Your Children Well: Parenting for Authentic Success*, "The happiest, most successful children have parents who ... do not do things for them that satisfy their own needs rather than the needs of the child."

Rapprochement – A child's sense of independence develops very quickly during the rapprochement subphase, from ages seventeen to twenty-four months. During this time, also known as the beginning of the "terrible twos," the child discovers self-sufficiency; learns to talk, including to say no; and identifies with his or her gender. Yet at the same time, a toddler's ever-growing awareness of his separateness from Mom causes him to feel more vulnerable. When you observe a rapprochement child, you'll see many contradictory behaviors, including increased movement away from the mother and demanding, coercive behavior that draws her back. This paradoxical tug-of-war is how the child assuages his anxiety about becoming more independent. Although he's exploring the world around him, he also needs to reassure himself that Mom is not far away. Mahler's observations led her to conclude that the child's impulse to discover the world includes the need to return to "home base" (Mom) for emotional refueling. Refueling is essential to the well-being of a newly separating child throughout the process of separation-individuation, particularly during the rapprochement subphase.

This is a period when the toddler most needs his mother to be emotionally available, and yet many mothers find it difficult to cope with their child's demanding, contradictory behavior during rapprochement. As the child's world widens, so does the psychological distance between mother and child. Both have to allow for the other's separateness. The child does this by being able to self-regulate his fears by calling up a mental image of Mom. That image provides comfort while still allowing the child a sense of his or her individuality as a separate person; Mahler called this "constancy." Mom's ability to make this transition is a reflection of her comfort with her own sense of Self, something that will directly influence her child's experiences with autonomy and intimacy later in life. "It is the inability to maintain parental boundaries," says Levine, "that most damages child development."

Consolidation of Individuality – The healthy unfolding of the child's psychological development ideally leads to consolidation of individuality by age three. Throughout the entire separation-individuation process, a child's sense of well-being grows from internalizing the love and support of his mother and developing a sense of himself as an independent person. The successful completion of symbiosis and separation-individuation allows a child to function as a separate Self even when he feels lonely for his mom or has angry thoughts about her. Adults who have experienced a successful psychological birth have the capacity to tolerate disappointments and frustrations by integrating and regulating their positive and negative emotions. Just as they saw their moms as whole people who sometimes made them angry, they also see their partners as independent Selves whom they continue to love even when they are dissatisfied with their actions.

"Throughout the entire separation-individuation process, a child's sense of well-being grows from internalizing the love and support of his mother and developing a sense of himself as an independent person."

Three Models

When a child's physical and emotional needs are met and successful symbiosis and individuation have taken place, he has experienced "good-enough" mothering, a phrase developed by pediatrician and psychoanalyst Donald Winnicott. Though it's impossible to be a perfect parent, a "good-enough mother" has provided her child with a feeling of being loved and wanted as well as giving the child a sense of trust and safety. Through healthy attachment, Mom establishes "the basis on which the child will form relationships with others; his sense of security about exploring the world; his resilience to stress; his ability to balance his emotions, make sense of his life, and create meaningful interpersonal relationships in the future," according to Drs. Marti Glenn, Jaelline Jaffe, and Jeanne Segal.

But what does less-than-good-enough mothering look like, and how does it reveal itself in adult relationships? In my practice I offer patients three models to show some basic variations on healthy separation and individuation as well as a model for the "good-enough" parent-child bond. Parenting can take innumerable forms, but these models illustrate some basic challenges to establishing a healthy bond between parent and child, challenges many people identify with. From there, I ask my patients if any of the three models strikes a chord with them. The adult scenarios that follow these examples give an idea of parallel situations in adulthood.

Model 1 Child – In this and following scenarios, we'll pretend we are observing a mom and her two-and-a-half-year-old child. Together they are working on a puzzle for toddlers that consists of large, geometrically shaped wooden pieces that fit into a board with the same shapes cut out of it.

In this case, the mother of the child is overprotective and highly invested in the child getting the puzzle pieces properly in their place. She anxiously watches the child working the puzzle and experiencing a healthy amount of frustration. After a few minutes, she just can't watch any longer. She interferes prematurely, taking the small hand that holds the puzzle piece and guiding it to the right place on the board. After essentially fitting the piece into its place herself, Mom begins praising the child. Her actions and praise give him a false sense of mastery and emphasize the dependence between herself and her toddler, a dependence that by this point in the child's development should be much less strong.

This is a child who will likely need a lot of reinforcement and nurturing later in life. What might that look like?

Model 1 Adult – The child, now a grown woman, is married to a successful businessman. For the last several years she's been a stay-at-home mom, but now that her youngest is about to start school, she's decided to get her real estate license. Today's the day of the exam. Anxious, she asks her husband to call her at 3:00 when the test is over so she can talk to him about how it went. Three o'clock comes and goes, but he doesn't call. Instead of picking up the phone herself, she starts to worry. Why hasn't he called? Has he forgotten? Doesn't he care about her and her future? Why didn't he support her more when she decided to go back to school for her license? Does he think being married to a real estate agent is beneath him? As she often does, the woman feels inadequate and insecure.

Model 2 Child – We're back to a different mother-child pair, again working a puzzle. This time, the mother is a law student, and while her child is working on the puzzle she is busy reading her textbooks in preparation for class. After a healthy amount of frustration, the child looks around, hoping for some guidance. However Mom is engrossed in her books and doesn't notice his cue that he needs help. He begins to whimper, but she doesn't look up. He'll have to master the puzzle without her.

As this child grows older, he may develop a sense of pseudo-independence. Even during times of need, he may not trust other people to be there for him, instead relying on himself to get through challenging situations alone. Let's take a look at how that might express itself in adulthood.

Model 2 Adult – Our Model 2 child, now a grown man, is up for an important job interview. His wife, excited about what this could mean for his career and their life together, offers her support. She tells him she'd be happy to take his best suit to the cleaners and buy him a new shirt for the interview, but he refuses, saying he'll do it himself. She asks if he would like to practice answering interview questions the night before. He says no. The day of the interview arrives, and she surprises him by picking him up in front of the building so he won't have to take the train home alone. Instead of being pleased, he's angry that she's there and refuses to talk about how the interview went on the drive home. His only comment is that he won't know if he got the job for another week, and would she please not ask him about it before then? As he often does, he rebuffs the intimacy and emotional connection his wife offers, as his early experiences with his mother cause him to mistrust the reliability of her offers.

Model 3 Child – As this child begins working the puzzle, the mother watches carefully. She is thinking in terms of the child's independence and autonomy. The toddler starts to get frustrated, but Mom lets him push himself a little further. Can he figure out how to do it alone? Eventually he looks around for help, and she steps in, realizing he is beyond his depth. She is neither overparenting nor parenting inadequately.

This mother knows the right balance between giving her child the instant gratification of Mom completing the puzzle for him and frustrating the child by not helping enough. She has exhibited that "the small challenges that start in infancy present the opportunity for successful failures," in other words, failures that your child can accept and grow from, as Madeline Levine describes them.

Model 3 Adult – The child, now a middle-aged man, heads off to a busy day of work while his wife goes in for her annual mammogram. Just after lunch, she calls to tell him she needs to talk to him, and asks if he could meet her for coffee even though she knows his afternoon is filled with meetings. Not hesitating for a moment, he says yes, hangs up, and moves his afternoon appointments to a later day. When he arrives at the coffee shop, he hugs her, sits down, and holds her hand as she begins to talk. Although he is frightened too, the man listens carefully and doesn't project his fears onto his wife. She tells him they've discovered a lump, and she may need a lumpectomy or even a mastectomy. He asks her what the next steps are and what she wants to do. He is supportive, loving, and encouraging. Though he must return to work to wrap up a few things, he lets her know he'll be home right afterward, and they can talk more then if she wants to, or leave the discussion for later. This man sees his wife as a separate individual who must make her own decisions, but someone he loves who needs emotional support—in other words, he supports his wife as his mother supported him.

---

*"Though it's impossible to be a perfect parent,
a 'good-enough mother' has provided her child with
a feeling of being loved and wanted as well as giving
the child a sense of trust and safety."*

A Conceptual Framework

By reviewing Mahler's basic theory of childhood development and illustrating what complete and incomplete psychological birth can look like, we now have a conceptual framework with which to understand the foundation for an adult's capacity to create and sustain successful relationships. This foundation is mirrored throughout life in our relationships with others; it manifests itself in every other human bond we make, so the separation-individuation model can also be applied to couples as they evolve through the stages of their relationship. It's precisely Dr. Mahler's concepts of complete and incomplete childhood development that have helped me understand the dynamics of my divorcing patients whose unresolved issues in their early development have contributed directly to their failed marriages.

In Chapter 4, we'll look at the striking parallels between the childhood stages of development as described by Mahler and the dynamics that exist between two marital partners as their relationship unfolds. In so doing, you can begin to make some preliminary connections between your early relationship with your mom (or primary caregiver) and the relationship with your former spouse. Since it's impossible to remember infancy, reflecting on your childhood memories of your mother's availability as a secure home base and her attunement to facilitating your growing independence will help you to see how those successes and frustrations played out in your marriage.

"This foundation is mirrored throughout life in our relationships with others; it manifests itself in every other human bond we make, so the separation-individuation model can also be applied to couples as they evolve through stages of their relationship."

Chapter 4

Underdeveloped Identity and the Divorce-Prone Relationship

To the extent that a person feels separate and whole, he or she also feels complete. As we explored in Chapter 3, a healthy mother-child bond facilitates that feeling of completion and ability to manage the stress, emotions, and insecurities we encounter in later relationships. Unfortunately, for a whole host of reasons, many people don't experience a complete psychological birth. Their mother or primary caregiver may have been depressed, withdrawn, preoccupied, anxious, or caught up in feelings of inadequacy during the child's early, psychologically formative years. Or, the parent may have had a difficult time learning the language between mother and child, aligning the child's needs too much with her own or unconsciously pushing the child away. In cases of abuse or neglect, the child may never have experienced the symbiotic relationship or stages of separation-individuation so necessary to establishing feelings of trust and safety in other relationships. There are many places where the mother-child relationship can go off course.

When it does, psychological development is hindered, and that can cause dependency issues later in life. Instead of having a strong sense of Self, adults who don't complete the separation-individuation process with their parent unconsciously seek to complete it with their partner. They use their partner as a kind of mirror to reassure or even define themselves. This kind of dependency creates an identity where losing your partner is tantamount to losing yourself.

Transferring Your Quest for Identity to Your Partner

There are lots of different ways incomplete psychological development in children can reveal itself in the relationships we have as adults. If you examine your former marriage honestly, you may begin to see patterns of behavior that reflect the need to focus outwardly, toward your partner, rather than inwardly, toward yourself and a strong sense of personal identity. Can you identify with the following behaviors?

- You looked to your spouse to figure out what you wanted or needed.

- You didn't have confidence in your ability to take care of yourself.

- You felt powerless to make changes in your life so you depended on your spouse to succeed.

- You felt your spouse needed to change in order for your marriage to get better.

- You found it hard to be alone with yourself.

- You worried about your spouse leaving you.

- You felt controlled and manipulated by your spouse's feelings.

- You did things to please your spouse even when you didn't want to.

- You believed you were not good enough.

- You relied on your spouse to take care of your needs.

- You wished your spouse loved you more and paid more attention to you.

- You manipulated, controlled, and complained when you didn't get your way.

"Instead of having a strong sense of Self, adults who don't complete the separation-individuation process with their parent unconsciously seek to complete it with their partner ... This kind of dependency creates an identity where losing your partner is tantamount to losing yourself."

By the same token, you may exhibit distancing rather than clinging behaviors, which also represent a lack of complete psychological development. Often, men and women with anxious or clingy behaviors pair with avoidant or distant partners in their attempt to create one "whole" person. Do any of these describe how you acted toward your former husband or wife?

- You were hypersensitive about your spouse controlling you.

- You had a strong need to be right.

- You expected your partner to be perfect.

- You often said no to your spouse's ideas.

- You became easily enraged at your spouse when your needs were unmet or you didn't get your way.

- You moved away from or rebelled against your spouse when he or she wanted to get close to you.

- Intimacy created anxiety.

- You resisted expressing your needs.

- You feared being consumed by your spouse's needs.

- You believed your spouse should treat you in special ways.

- You acted like a bully.

Depending on our unique individual histories, the patterns of behavior we develop to manage our world and our relationships vary. Looking back to the models given in Chapter 3, you'll see a couple of examples of outwardly focused behaviors learned in early childhood, one anxious and the other avoidant. You'll also see how those behaviors played themselves out in adulthood, resulting in dependent or incomplete relationships.

If you see yourself in those models, or in the behaviors listed above, don't despair. Although these patterns may be hard habits to break, they are not set in stone. Sometimes it's easier to remain trapped in the thinking that you are who you are, but psychological development continues into adult life, albeit at a slower pace than in childhood. What you do to enhance that development can lead to a healthier Self and more rewarding relationships.

Understanding your own developmental history and how it affects your way of interacting with others, especially how it affected your marriage, is the first step. Looking at your past—both your early childhood and your adult relationships—and understanding its deficiencies can help you open up to the possibility of approaching life from a position of greater security. You don't have to get stuck in a place of being dependent on another person to tell you who you are—or of being that demanding person others eventually rebel against.

"If you examine your former marriage honestly, you may begin to see patterns of behavior that reflect the need to focus outwardly, toward your partner, rather than inwardly, toward yourself and a strong sense of personal identity."

The Parallels between Childhood Identity Formation and How Relationships Unfold

Drs. Ellen Bader and Peter Pearson first identified the parallels between Margaret Mahler's developmental theory on childhood identity formation and the progression couples go through in relationships. Their ground-breaking book, *In Quest of the Mythical Mate*, led to new ways of understanding how couples interact based on early childhood experiences, and from that, offered new ways of helping partners improve their current and future relationships. Their model is also extremely helpful for individuals considering, experiencing, or having gone through divorce. Examining and understanding your history with your former spouse from a developmental standpoint, though it won't fix the defunct marriage, will provide clarity and a healthy foundation for new partnerships.

Bader and Pearson pointed out that from those early, heady days of romance through the changes and challenges that ensue in marriage, couples experience stages that parallel the symbiosis, differentiation, practicing, rapprochement, and mutual interdependence of childhood. As adults, these stages are more complex and less rigidly attached to time spans, but the similarities are nonetheless remarkable.

Symbiosis – During the symbiotic stage in infancy, a newborn child is filled up with the bliss of his mother's unconditional love. The boundaries between mother and child are more or less nonexistent. Mothers have described the intimate experience with their babies during symbiosis as a time when they lose their usual way of interacting with the world. Their focus on their child is unwavering, and if boundaries are forced between the two, both Mom and baby will experience enormous pain and frustration.

The same situation exists early in romantic relationships. Think back to the early days with your soon-to-be spouse. During that symbiotic stage, when you were "crazy in love" with each other, you were a merged pair. Life was blissful, and you most likely wanted to spend all your time with your partner, to the exclusion of other people and activities that were important to you before you met your newfound love. The two of you focused on your similarities, and overlooked or ignored your differences. Neither one wanted to rock the boat by being demanding or selfish, spending time with others, or working or playing apart when you could be together. In many people's eyes, this stage of a relationship represents perfect love—just like they've seen in the movies.

However, during the symbiotic phase of relationships, the picture you have of one another is not whole. In the same way mothers form impressions of their babies during symbiosis, people in the early stages of love define their partners by the fantasies they've created about them in addition to the actual cues they get from one another. There is often a feeling that you can read each other's minds, that you think and feel in the same way, and when differences are noticed, they are often looked upon lovingly rather than as points of contention.

In ways very similar to the early mother-child bond, the attachment that people form with one another during this stage becomes the foundation of their relationship. Each enjoys this nurturing time; as Bader and Pearson note, "The child inside them feels responded to on so many levels that it makes it easy to give unconditionally." The attention, compliments, and physical excitement are intoxicating.

If each person feels fulfilled by the bond they have established during symbiosis, they start their relationship off on solid ground. In the healthiest situations, this foundation allows them to move on to the next stage: differentiation.

Differentiation – Just as in the mother/child pair, where each eventually needs greater independence, adults too need to express their individuality apart from the romantic bond as they move away from symbiosis.

The urge to express your individuality apart from your romantic partner happens instinctively, in the same way no one has to tell a baby when it's time to move beyond the comfort of his mother's lap. One or both partners begin to feel the need to have more private time, enjoy dinner with a friend rather than a routine couple's night at home, or spend extra time at the office to get a jump on a big project. For the first time, the relationship begins to look less like a "we" and more like two "I's." Yet the urge toward independence is not complete; despite these forays toward separateness, the differentiating couple's investment is still primarily in the relationship.

During differentiation, in addition to needing some time on your own, a clearer picture of who your partner is begins to emerge. You absorb more fully the things that set you apart: differences in politics, religion, ties to family and work, goals for children, careers, and retirement, approaches to money. Things you saw as adorable quirks early in the relationship may begin to frustrate or bother you. Couples often experience their first arguments at this stage. Guilt often accompanies the need to turn to individual pursuits, and jealousy can ensue if one of the two partners wants to maintain symbiosis.

If partners don't differentiate simultaneously—and few do—this is the first phase of a relationship in which an imbalance exists. Differentiation is therefore cause for concern in the partner who is not ready to move away from the bliss of symbiosis. For the partner who is ready, self-exploration beckons, and the plea to remain merged with another can feel smothering.

"You don't have to get stuck in a place of being dependent on another person to tell you who you are."

For individuals left behind in this imbalanced scenario, the first signs of differentiation can be too threatening to endure. Symbiotically enmeshed individuals see the need for their partner to do things alone as a sign that the relationship is over. Using cultural models from the media as their guide, these people may define love as that blissful initial state, so when differences between two people start to show, they think love is through. Consider what happened in Kim Kardashian's marriage to Kris Humphreys. After a fairy tale $10 million wedding, they remained married for only 72 days, divorcing when the complexities of married life overwhelmed their earlier symbiosis.

In the normal course of events, couples may experience grief at having to let go of the euphoria of their early love, but they find differentiation to be a worthwhile challenge, which then moves on to the practicing stage.

Practicing – For children, practicing is an exciting time when full-on exploration of the world begins. The practicing child, with newly developed motor skills and the security of his mother's love, experiences elation in exercising his unique capabilities. In the best-case scenario, his continuing trust in his mother's availability and her comfort, coupled with his burgeoning independence, allow him to explore his world's novelty freely. In other instances, Mom's feelings of inadequacy or rejection during her child's practicing stage cause her to smother him or otherwise inhibit his growth as an individual.

In adult relationships, though partners do sometimes encourage and delight in their partner's practicing, more often they feel threatened or confused by it. According to Bader and Pearson, the onset of practicing occurs when one or both partners shift energy away from the romantic bond to explore independent activities and people outside of the relationship. In other words, the search for or reestablishment of their individual identity becomes paramount. Unlike during the differentiation phase, when the emphasis is still on joint activities and mutual satisfaction, during the practicing phase one or both individuals' energy becomes withdrawn from the relationship and refocused into new, self-directed pursuits. If there is an imbalance during this period, where one of the partners is focused on his or her "I" and personal growth and the other is primarily intent on nurturing the "we" of an earlier stage, practicing becomes a particularly rocky time.

During this phase there is usually a minimizing of emotional contact between the partners and an increase in conflict. Though a balance needs to be struck between conflicting individual desires, compromise can be difficult. Bader and Pearson note that this is a time when couples must develop an effective fighting style. If they don't, the neglected party may feel like their partner is falling out of love with them, and in response the accused, who is highly protective of his or her individuality, can feel smothered and engulfed. Interestingly, though years may have passed since the relationship began, during the practicing phase partners must get to know one another as individual people with individual viewpoints and needs, and find out if and how those differences can be managed.

Rapprochement – In contrast to the practicing phase, where the child is focused on his individual mastery and autonomy, rapprochement brings about some interesting developments in a child's psychology. By the end of this phase, if the child has had "good-enough" parenting, he is comforted by the idea of his mother, not only by her presence, and he begins to view her empathetically. Mom serves as his "home base"—he knows she is there for him and that he can rely on her—and this gives him a sense of constancy that allows him to function well in the larger world. He also begins to recognize that others have needs separate from his own, and can balance their needs with his. When a child has had less than "good-enough" parenting, however—for example if his mother is depressed or volatile— there is less opportunity for the rich emotional interactions necessary for empathy and mature relationships.

Rapprochement couples experience the same types of psychological developments. If they have made it past practicing to this stage, they have come to recognize and honor the need for their partner's expressions of independence while simultaneously seeking more closeness and intimacy with them without the fear of losing their own individuality. They can easily resolve their conflicts and differences without the power struggles of earlier stages. Their developed identities allow them to give to the other even when it is not convenient. In the same way a psychologically developed child feels constancy toward his mother and self-assured in his own abilities, rapprochement couples feel secure as individuals in part because of the love and support they get from their relationship. In sum, they are committed to themselves and to the partnership; their relationship consists of two people and the union that brings them together.

Conflict and the "See-Saw" Effect

There are two situations that typically signal the beginning of problems in a relationship. Most common is an imbalance between how each individual within a couple progresses through the relationship's stages of development. One partner may be hanging on to symbiosis while the other moves into differentiation. A wife may be in the practicing phase, taking on more responsibilities at work and spending additional hours at the office, while the husband wants her to spend more time with him in the cozy nest they've created together, a blissful, symbiotic place where the outside world seems far away. Or the female counterpart in the relationship may have settled into rapprochement, feeling content in her individuality as well as the partnership, while her spouse is still struggling to define himself as separate, and spends lots of time with others in activities she's not included in. Bader and Pearson call this imbalance the "see-saw" effect, and note that when the see-saw effect is in play, there tends to be a struggle for balance.

Interestingly, the two psychiatrists have never counseled couples who are more than two stages apart in their developmental process. Occasionally, however, they have encountered individuals stuck together in one stage for too long, and their stasis has become destructive. Most typically, stuck couples are caught in symbiosis, and have shut out the outside world in order to try to maintain "perfect love" as they see it.

"Examining and understanding your history with your former spouse from a developmental standpoint, though it won't fix the defunct marriage, will provide clarity and a healthy foundation for new partnerships."

You and Me against the World

Partners caught in symbiosis tend to do everything together, have very few friends outside the relationship, have not developed an effective fighting style and thus revert to childlike behavior, and often don't have a "future focus" in which they create goals for themselves as individuals as well as for themselves as a couple. Symbiotically enmeshed individuals typically have a poor sense of Self that stems from childhood. Their psychological development was incomplete, and so they hope to make up for their lack of a healthy mother-child bond in their marriage.

I rarely see this sort of couple in my practice. Typically, they have an unspoken agreement to maintain the status quo. As Drs. Barry and Janae Weinhold say in their book *Breaking Free of the Co-Dependency Trap*, "Because both partners lacked secure bonding in early childhood, neither is free to feel or act independently of the other, so they stick together like glue … The relationship cannot grow because the goal is never conscious or spoken."

But occasionally, one of the members of a symbiotic couple will wish to break free from the marriage suddenly and without explanation, leaving behind a spouse who thought everything in the relationship was perfect, until that eventful day.

The Symbiotic-Symbiotic Couple – My patient Heather went through just that situation. After five years of what she considered a blissful marriage, Heather's spouse Dave left her abruptly and refused to talk about why. "We wanted to do everything together throughout our marriage," Heather told me during our first meeting. "It was like an extended honeymoon. I'd never had sex like that before. Everyone who knew us thought we were the perfect couple. I have no idea what happened."

Both Heather and Dave had had difficult childhoods. Heather's parents divorced soon after her birth, and her mother was unequipped to take care of her. From early infancy, Heather lived with a variety of relatives—her grandmother, an aunt, her father and his new wife. None gave her the attention she needed as a small child, and she was often left to play alone. From high school forward, she had a series of serious boyfriends, but most found her too needy and eventually broke it off. With Dave, she thought she had found her one true love, someone who would give her constant attention, compliments, and physical expressions of his adoration.

Dave grew up the youngest son in a large, financially strapped family. Both parents worked, and so Dave was often left in the care of his older siblings. He resented the fact that most of his clothing was hand-me-downs, that even though he was a good student his parents could not afford to send him to college, and that his mother didn't have much time for him.

With Heather, things were different. She lavished him with gifts, attention, and saw his potential to make something of his life. For a while, he couldn't believe his good luck. Then, he began to feel smothered.

What Heather didn't understand was that although the romance was real, it was temporary. She was "in love," but only with her idealized version of Dave. In describing her ex-husband, it was clear that Heather held on to fantasies about Dave that were not reflective of reality. She spoke of him as being perfect, the only man she could ever love, someone without faults who shared hopes and dreams identical to her own.

Typical of couples in the symbiotic stage who experience their mates as larger-than-life, Heather became temporarily blinded to the reality of who Dave really was. She only felt alive if Dave was paying attention to her, and couldn't understand why he didn't feel the same way, why he needed to exist apart from their "we." Her emotional dependency on Dave, her continuous complaints that he was ignoring her and not meeting her needs, and her expectation that he provide her with his undivided attention caused Dave to feel suffocated and victimized. Though his departure without explanation was unfair to Heather and to the marriage, it made one thing perfectly clear: he needed out.

"If partners don't differentiate simultaneously— and few do—this is the first phase of a relationship in which an imbalance exists."

Developmental Imbalance

More often, my patients divorce because they have experienced an imbalance in the relationship they were not equipped to handle. After reviewing the series of events that led to the divorce, we take a close look at their underlying childhood influences, and the see-saw effect that signaled problems in the marriage. Using Bader and Pearson's diagnostic terms for couples at different stages, let's take a look at some of the problems that can ensue.

The Symbiotic-Differentiating Couple – Rarely do individuals in a couple progress from symbiosis to differentiation at the same time. Typically, one is ready to move forward and the other is not. It can be a destabilizing situation, to say the least. That's exactly what happened to Rochelle, who contacted me early in her marriage to Richie because she was contemplating separation and wanted more clarity on her feelings.

After a glorious honeymoon in Africa, the couple had reluctantly returned to their professional lives in New York City. Richie, an attorney with the City of New York, loved his work and although he felt sad to leave Rochelle at the start of each workday, he eagerly tackled his meetings with his colleagues and clients. Rochelle, on the other hand, spent her days at home writing her dissertation, and she could hardly wait until Richie walked through the door every evening so she could spend what remained of the day cuddling with him. While Richie, too, was excited to see Rochelle, the stress of his work left him needing to unwind for a bit by himself before settling in with her.

It is not difficult to see that the harmony of the symbiotic honeymoon period had become imbalanced for Richie and Rochelle. Rochelle began to grieve that "the thrill was gone." Her disappointment in Richie's need for space (differentiation) led her to outbursts of anger regarding his "selfishness." They still spent plenty of time together, but Rochelle was beginning to wonder what the future would look like if Richie were willing to turn his focus away from their marriage so soon after the wedding day.

As Rochelle described her early home life to me, the reasons for her anxiety became clearer. Rochelle had three sisters, and her parents had encouraged sameness among them. Though they each had their own talents, the girls worked hard to minimize their differences in order to please their mother and father. If one of the girls wanted to go off and do something alone, the parents protested; on vacations, for example, the only sanctioned activities were things the family agreed to do as a unit. So when Rochelle was singled out by Richie as someone special and unique, she felt elated to have the spotlight finally focused on her. Never before had she been paid so much attention, and it was wonderful. Then other demands in Richie's life pulled him away from her, and that special attention waned. In light of Rochelle's history, her anxiety in reaction to Richie's reasonable needs was understandable.

What our work enabled Rochelle to see was that differentiation, for both of them, was a normal and natural progression in their relationship. Happily, Richie's inner sense of security enabled him to be compassionate and reassuring to her, which in turn allowed her to understand his fatigue and need for time alone after work. In the end, the safety of their bond, which was established in the symbiotic period, enabled them to effectively respond to one another's feelings in a way that supported increasing differentiation.

The Differentiating-Practicing Couple – The practicing phase of a relationship can be the hardest, and bring about the most conflict. Practicing is a time when the energy of individuals in a relationship is shifted to outward pursuits, and the resulting stress on the marriage can be enormous.

A couple I am very fond of, Lynne and Frank, typify the conflicts of the practicing stage. Both were very competent financial analysts, and had managed differentiation beautifully. But when Lynne put aside her career to raise their only child and Frank became hyper-focused on his career, sparks began to fly.

Lynne's mom was also a professional woman, and had raised five children, returning to work after each child. That left Lynne competing for attention with her mother's career as well as her siblings, and she often felt neglected. Frank, a very kind and considerate man, loved Lynne but after the "honeymoon" of their first years together and the birth of their daughter, he began to practice with increasing intensity. To Lynne, it appeared that the marriage took second place to Frank's career—just as she had felt during childhood that her needs took second place to her mom's busy life. Lynne's insecurity caused her to "ice out" Frank, which in turn alienated him. Their relationship descended into repeated power struggles, and soon they looked to me for help. Despite their conflicts, which were mainly provoked by Lynne's deeply rooted fears of abandonment, Lynne and Frank's marriage prevailed. During the course of our counseling, Lynne took greater ownership of her fears and was able to connect them to her past rather than directing them to Frank. Frank, in turn, developed a greater understanding of Lynne's withdrawals, which helped him to respond less emotionally to them.

The Rapprochement Couple – Rapprochement is the sign of a well-developed couple, but that doesn't mean there won't be conflict. During the rapprochement phase, there is still room for deeper intimacy and a more developed sense of constancy; in other words, the ability to manage closeness and distance with ease.

Chris and Susan exemplify this developmental phase to a T. In their case, conflict became an opportunity for intimacy. About eight years into their marriage, Susan, a pediatrician, was invited to join a practice in a city about four hours from their home, a job that would catapult her career. Chris loved life in the country and did not have the option to relocate. The situation was complicated by the fact that they had two young children and neither Chris nor Susan was open to living apart from them. As you can imagine, there were many heated discussions between them in which old hurts and wounds surfaced. Both Susan and Chris came from broken families and were threatened by the prospect of the family being fragmented.

But more important than the context of the conflict's resolution was how Chris and Susan managed their differences. As clearly defined, separate-but-equal individuals, each was able to identify his or her respective needs and ask for what they wanted. Together, they shared their feelings about the problem at hand and how the different options would affect the marriage. They listened closely to each other's perceptions and concerns and tried hard not to defend or blame. Ultimately, they were able to negotiate their differences and find a solution that worked for the whole family. Despite the initial resistance to spending time away from the children, Susan realized that an accommodation needed to be made by her in order to resolve the impasse. Theirs is an excellent example of the kinds of sacrifices that good partners must willingly make for the integrity of the marriage.

"The urge to express your individuality apart from your romantic partner happens instinctively, in the same way no one has to tell a baby when it's time to move beyond the comfort of his mother's lap."

For the rapprochement couple, whose individual identities are securely defined, conflict is not inherently bad. Unlike with differentiating or practicing couples, it doesn't have to be associated with aggression and power plays. Rapprochement is a time when feelings, however unpleasant, can be expressed in a direct, healthy fashion so that closeness results. In lieu of perceiving an argument as a competition to be won, each partner considers the welfare of the other as a necessary factor in a satisfactory resolution. A rapprochement couple may best be thought of as players on the same team.

* * *

Looking back over your own marriage with these examples and definitions in mind, you are probably analyzing it according to Mahler's stages of separation and individuation. Did clinging to symbiosis cause conflict with a differentiating or practicing partner? Were you unable to successfully express yourself as an individual and still find strength and comfort in the love of your partner?

Concepts of individuality and togetherness as they exist in a marriage take on a new meaning in light of this larger picture. Although it may seem paradoxical, having a successful partnership necessitates having a clear sense of You. No matter what your age, you have to grow up and take responsibility for your dependencies, your complexities, and your fears, and develop the courage to relinquish blaming your spouse for your failures.

In the next chapter, we'll take a look at how to develop your underdeveloped "I" to begin that journey.

Chapter 5

Exploring Your
Underdeveloped "I"

In a perfect world, everyone would come through the separation-individuation process with a fully developed sense of Self.
Parenting during those first three critical years would have been
highly successful because your mother or primary caretaker would
have done all the right things: modeled behavior based on her
own psychological independence; met your needs for nurturing,
protection, physical touch, and emotional attunement; accepted
you for who you are, not who she wanted you to be; supported
your expression of independent thoughts, feelings, and actions;
encouraged you to explore your world; and taught you to ask
directly for what you wanted rather than control others in order
to meet your needs.

Sadly, that experience is not a reflection of most people's
reality. Authors Janae and Barry Weinhold, in their books *The
Flight from Intimacy* and *Breaking Free of the Co-Dependency
Trap*, assert that 98 percent of people have experienced some
level of developmental trauma brought about by shortcomings
of the mother-child bond. In most cases, our mothers (or other
primary caregivers) didn't cause that trauma intentionally. They
were just mimicking what they knew from their own childhood
experience and their parents' incomplete separation-individuation behavior, and were not able to distinguish dysfunctional

interactions from healthy ones. Children in particular have a hard time knowing what healthy interactions look like, but adults and parents have that same trouble as well, especially if they grew up with less-than-perfect parenting themselves.

"Ninety-eight percent of people have experienced some level of developmental trauma brought about by shortcomings of the mother-child bond."

Two Responses

The inadequacies most of us experience before age three can result in two kinds of maladaptive behavior: codependency, which expresses itself as low self-esteem, clinginess, and/or depression, among other responses, and counter-dependency, which is often revealed in self-centeredness, avoidance of intimacy, and/or a controlling nature. Not every therapist uses these labels for behavioral patterns, and some break these two categories down further, but generally people who did not complete their development in childhood are, to various extents, either predisposed to immature dependencies (anxious) or avoid dependence on others (avoidant). How much adult relationships are influenced by the unmet needs of childhood varies greatly, depending on how much and at what stage each individual's development was interrupted. For some people, anxious or avoidant tendencies are manageable; for others, they impact relationships in damaging ways.

The good news is, codependency and counter-dependency are not permanent, incurable conditions. As the Weinholds and many other therapists emphasize, developmental completion can occur in adulthood: it's a matter of understanding the gaps in your early development and doing the work to repair them, either on your own or with a therapist.

Maladaptive Behaviors

Without experiencing a healthy psychological birth or understanding the separation-individuation process as adults, the way most people cope with developmental gaps is through maladaptive behaviors. Children absorb how their primary caregivers interact with them, and they also watch their parents to see how they interact with one another, eventually adopting the behaviors that are modeled or encouraged. As psychologist Randi Gunther says in her book *Relationship Saboteurs*, "Familiarity is a powerful magnet. It will draw people to re-create what they were taught, even if those lessons were unfulfilling or painful."

Consider the scenarios I gave in the "Three Models" section of Chapter 3. If a child is smothered and not allowed to individuate, the result is an adult who is highly dependent on others, has difficulty with boundaries, feels insecure and incompetent, and has a hard time succeeding in the world. If a child is left to fend for himself when he needs guidance and praise in order to learn, he compensates by putting on a front that he is strong and secure, blames instead of taking responsibility for his own failings, controls or victimizes others, and keeps intimacy at bay.

These coping behaviors play out in their rawest form during marriage. In a marital union, unlike in any other adult relationship, individuals seek an attachment that will fulfill the child inside them who is looking for absolute security, an identity, self-esteem, unwavering support, and fulfillment. Individuals on the opposite sides of the spectrum are often drawn to one another because of this: the clingy, insecure man or woman wants a counterpart who is invulnerable, self-assured, and competent. Instead, he or she may end up with someone who has a false sense of Self, is cut off from their feelings, and seeks to control rather than get close. Neither an anxious nor a falsely confident person can find the completion they are looking for from a partner who manages the world from an equally incomplete but opposite approach. So in the end, two halves don't end up making a whole. The wholeness needs to come from within.

> "Developmental completion can occur in adulthood: it's a matter of understanding the gaps in your early development and doing the work to repair them, either on your own or with a therapist."

A Step-by-Step Process to Exploring Your Underdeveloped "I"

Changing the behaviors you've learned or adopted from the time you were a child is frightening. Even when you know those behaviors aren't effective, they are a part of who you are.

Your reactions of feeling insecure, smothered, marginalized, undermined, defensive, or manipulated by your partner are valid responses based on what your parents taught you about interacting with others. And your partner, coming into the relationship with his or her own set of maladaptive behaviors, feels legitimized by his or her reactions too. It's easy to see others as the problem, not you.

As understandable and legitimate as that defensive stance may be, it's time to take an objective view. Almost all of us come into adult relationships with baggage from our childhood, so we need to take a good, hard look at the roots of our relationship coping skills so we can develop beyond them. It's a revolutionary but necessary process. Randi Gunther says it best: "You have to learn to trust in a future you cannot know, have faith in your own capabilities ... and find the strength within yourself to leave your insecurities behind." This step-by-step process can help.

Step 1: Exploring the Origins of Your Insecurities: The first step in completing your developmental process is to look at the separation-individuation process you experienced as a child. Based on the behaviors listed at the beginning of Chapter 4 and the case studies that followed, you may already have an idea of your current dependencies. Where did those coping behaviors come from? This first exercise will help you clarify how interactions with your primary caregiver established an attachment style that has carried through to your adult life, specifically your marriage. By spending thoughtful time considering your earliest memories, you can begin to pinpoint the deficits from your particular mother-child matrix.

Exercise 1: Impactful Childhood Memories

Begin by writing down three of your earliest and most impactful memories that involve your mother or primary caregiver. Give as much detail as possible: the setting, your state of mind, your reaction to the incident, how you perceived your parent, how you perceived yourself, whether other people were there and their reactions, and what you took away from that experience.

Now ask yourself these questions:

1. How do those memories make you feel today (happy, sad, angry, powerful, weak, loved, smothered, ignored, etc.)?

2. How would you categorize the way your parent interacted with you in those memories (nurturing, dismissive, loving, uninvolved, overinvolved, etc.)?

3. How would you label your childhood self in those situations (confident, shy, fearful, outgoing, etc.)?

4. Why do you think these particular memories stand out for you? Is there a common thread?

5. If you could change what happened for the person you were then, how would you change it? How would you change the actions of your primary caregiver?

"In a marital union, unlike in any other adult relationship, individuals seek an attachment that will fulfill the child inside them who is looking for absolute security, an identity, self-esteem, unwavering support, and fulfillment."

Exercise 2: Patterns in the Mother-Child Relationship

Vivid memories are just one way we can identify our attachment style and how it was influenced by our primary caregiver during our earliest years. Identifying patterns in our ongoing interactions with our mother during childhood can further hone in on deficits in early psychological development. The next exercise can help you do just that.

2a: Based on a scale of 1–5, with 1 being "not true" and 5 being "very true," respond to the following statements:

1. My primary caregiver was always at my elbow, ready to help with a project or homework.

2. I relied on others to make me feel good, even though I had a hard time believing their praise.

3. I was fearful of the world, constantly using my parent as a buffer between me and the things that frightened me.

4. I was labeled "shy," "quiet," "fearful," and/or "needy."

5. My mother would make excuses for me, stating that I was "sensitive."

6. I tried never to "rock the boat," accepting even unpleasant situations quietly.

7. When playing with other children, I followed their lead rather than suggesting things I wanted to do or games I wanted to play.

8. If I was frightened of something new, my mother never pressed me to try it.

9. I felt invisible around others, even when I had something to contribute.

10. I hated being the center of attention.

Scoring: Tally up the entire column. The following scale can help you determine your attachment style.

Score 40–50 = anxious or codependent tendencies
Score 10–20 = avoidant or counter-dependent tendencies
Score 20–30 = secure or highly consolidated tendencies

2b: Based on a scale of 1–5, with 1 being "not true" and 5 being "very true," respond to the following statements:

1. My primary caregiver pushed me to do things on my own, even when I needed her help and asked for it.

2. I relied on myself to feel nurtured.

3. I often felt abandoned or let down because my caretaker was consumed with work/other family members/illness/other.

4. I always wanted to do things on my own as a child, pushing adults away when they tried to help.

5. The adults in my life treated me like I was a little adult.

6. I liked to "run the show" with other children and even adults.

7. I spent a lot of time alone as a child, entertaining myself.

8. I was considered a bully, and liked to pick fights.

9. Even as a child, I could sweet talk people into doing things my way.

10. I was the first person to try new things, and brag about how well I did them.

Scoring: Tally up the entire column. The following scale can help you determine your attachment style.

Score 40–50 = avoidant or counter-dependent tendencies
Score 20-30 = secure or highly consolidated tendencies
Score 10–20 = anxious or codependent tendencies

Step 2: Defining Adult Relationship Patterns: The next step in the process of developing your undeveloped "I" is seeing your adult relationships in light of the mother-child experience. The way you interacted with your ex-spouse defines patterns that give shape to the unfinished business of your childhood. Seeing those patterns clearly is essential to completing your development, and comparing childhood and adult behaviors illuminates those patterns. With that in mind, let's revisit our earlier exercise, this time considering memories from your marriage.

Exercise 3: Impactful Memories from Your Marriage

Write down three impactful memories you feel best represent your relationship with your ex-spouse. Give as much detail as possible: the setting, your state of mind, your reaction to the incident, how you perceived your spouse, how you perceived yourself, whether other people were there and their reactions, and what you took away from that experience.

Ask yourself the same questions used for the first exercise:

1. How do those memories make you feel today
    (happy, sad, angry, powerful, weak, loved,
    smothered, ignored, etc.)?

2. How would you categorize the way your spouse
    interacted with you in those memories (nurturing,
    dismissive, loving, uninvolved, overinvolved, etc.)?

3. How would you label yourself in those situations
    (confident, shy, fearful, outgoing, etc.)?

4. Why do you think these particular memories stand
    out for you? Is there a common thread?

5. If you could change what happened for the person
    you were then, how would you change it—or would
    you leave it unchanged? How would you change
    your spouse's behavior?

You may be surprised to see the parallels between this exercise
and its partner from earlier in the chapter. Since incomplete
development seeks completion in close relationships, your unmet
needs for unconditional love, nurturing, protection, and trust
were probably recycled from your childhood into your marriage,
ultimately leaving you with the feeling that you could not
function maturely and effectively without your partner's help.

"Almost all of us come into adult relationships
with baggage from our childhood, so we need to
take a good, hard look at the roots of our relationship
coping skills so we can develop beyond them."

Exercise 4: Seeing Yourself through Other People's Eyes

Being objective about your behaviors can be very difficult, especially when you're hurting. But in order to leave your insecurities and ineffectual coping mechanisms behind, you have to see yourself through other people's eyes, not as a way of judging yourself, but to accept the past and move on to healthier relationships in the future. The next exercise can help you look at your past relationships more clearly.

Answer the following questions as honestly as you can, without placing blame on others or yourself.

1. If you were to survey the men or women with whom you've had relationships, how would they define you? List both the positive and negative attributes they might apply.

2. When you are feeling frightened or defensive, what are your go-to reactions? It is helpful to think about your "fight or flight" behavior at a time when you are feeling calm and can view it from another person's shoes.

3. What are the behaviors you see in yourself that reflect the way your parents interacted with you as

a child or the way they interacted with one another? Name both good and bad.

4. What are the behaviors you turn to even when you know they are not effective? These may be behaviors you repeatedly apologize for or are accused of exhibiting: being clingy, angry, untrustworthy, distant, etc.

5. If you were to be involved with someone who behaved as you do under stressful conditions, what would you think about their behavior?

From your answers, think about how you would categorize your common reactions. Are you fearful, clingy, unsure of yourself? Do you exhibit low self-esteem, the need for constant reassurance? Or do you tend to interact with people by fighting back, insisting you are right, dismissing their feelings, or always wanting to be the center of attention? Seeing yourself objectively as anxious or avoidant is the first step in finding new ways to interact with others.

Step 3: Defining Behaviors That You Want to Develop or Change: Now that you have explored/identified the parallels between your early development and its impact on your marriage, what behaviors do you think you need to develop or change in order to move forward in your relationships? Defining them on paper is the first step toward action.

Exercise 5: Where Do I Grow From Here?

List behaviors that you feel need developing or that you would like to change. As much as is possible, do this without judgment. Growth and personal development happen throughout life. Defining what you want to work on is a sign of your evolving sense of Self and a positive step.

Step 4: Exploring Who You Are as an Individual: Getting to know the child you were and how that person relates to the adult you have become is not just about pinpointing your developmental deficits and planning for change, however. It's also about seeing yourself as a whole person, recognizing the things you love about yourself as well as the things you want to work on. In order to become an adult for your internal child, you need to explore who you are honestly, comprehensively, and lovingly. Carl Jung believed this sort of exploration could only come in midlife, and the "gnosis," or knowledge, that arises from such self-contemplation would yield a spiritual rebirth that would set the human heart free.

One way to begin that journey is to really think about who you are and what you want, separate from the influences of any other relationship in your life, past or present.

Exercise 6: Getting In Touch With Who You Are

Below are some incomplete sentences that, if you finish them spontaneously and frankly, will put you in touch with basic aspects of your Self.

1. I feel happiest when …
2. I believe in …

3. What I like most about a person is …
4. I always …
5. I get angry when …
6. One thing I want to accomplish is …
7. What I like most about myself is …
8. I hate it when …
9. I feel untrue to myself when …
10. I feel weakest when …
11. When I am alone I feel …
12. I was the type of child who …
13. I feel strongest when …
14. On a beautiful day, I like to …
15. My favorite pastime is …
16. If my relationship with_____ were to end I would …

Even though you may not like the way you completed some of the sentences, the person who answered them is YOU. This means that you are a Self who has feelings, opinions, and desires and is not dependent on your spouse or anyone else to tell you who you are. If there are aspects of your identity that you don't like, you can explore how you came to be who you are and then begin the hard but rewarding work of changing yourself. But never forget to love yourself in the process, especially for taking on this difficult challenge.

In the absence of another person, either a parent or a spouse who will "refuel" you and provide you with a sense of constancy so you are capable of tackling the world, you must do that for yourself. In the next chapter, we'll explore tools and techniques for change that can help you on your journey.

"Since incomplete development seeks completion in close relationships, your unmet needs for unconditional love, nurturing, protection, and trust were probably recycled from your childhood into your marriage, ultimately leaving you with the feeling that you could not function maturely and effectively without your partner's help."

Chapter 6

Taking the Steps
Toward Change

In the last chapter you took an honest look at the ways you learned to interact as a child and how those coping mechanisms played out in your adult marital relationship. With the information you have read and the exercises you've worked through, you are gaining a clearer awareness of your own unique separation-individuation process, its deficits, and the effects those shortfalls had on your subsequent relationships, specifically your vulnerability, your imperfections, and your dependency needs. Increased knowledge about yourself and your problem behaviors raises your consciousness and is the primary step toward making changes.

It is also a scary step. No matter what the behavioral influences that contributed to your divorce, facing them in order to heal and move forward after your marriage ends is frightening. The future is uncertain, self-doubt may consume you, and you may feel stuck in the way you navigated relationships in the past. It's not unlike the time when a toddler begins to establish his identity as a Self separate from his mother and separation anxiety rears its worrisome head. After divorce, that same fear reappears—but with one big difference: Unlike the developing child who can be safely united with his mother after exploring the world on his own, divorcing adults have no rescuers, no Mommy or Daddy who can protect them when anxiety about developing independence takes over.

"Increased knowledge about yourself and your problem behaviors raises your consciousness and is the primary step toward making changes."

During marriage, there is the assumption, conscious or unconscious, that you can be "saved" by your spouse. When a marriage dissolves, that safe harbor is lost with it. For many, divorce is like being on a boat that is lost at sea, with no land in sight. One of my divorcing patients expressed her loss using that very metaphor: "I am losing my safe haven, my anchor, my rock." If your value and worth depend on your attachment to your spouse, it can be very frightening to envision life without him or her. My patient, like you, had two options: jump ship or sail on.

However shaky you may feel, the inescapable demand of your post-divorce journey is that you shift your focus from the expectation that your spouse will provide you with happiness and security to the reality of living more honestly with yourself. In order to change, grow, heal, and rebuild your faltering identity, you must muster the courage to take responsibility for your own life and your unfinished individuation. Like the toddler who is faced with the developmental imperative of separating from his mother, you must also confront your dependencies and fears.

Exercise 1: What Do You Fear?

The first step is defining those fears and the dependencies that underlie them. In this next exercise, I have listed fears common to those facing divorce. See how many strike a chord with you, and add any that are not listed here.

1. I fear being alone.
2. I fear not being able to handle my finances.
3. I fear not providing my children with the structure and guidance they need.
4. I fear that I can't provide for my family on my own.
5. I fear that I am not lovable.
6. I fear commitment.
7. I fear being smothered in a relationship.
8. I fear that I cannot handle day-to-day responsibilities on my own.
9. I fear that I am too distant to ever attract another partner.
10. I fear that I am too smothering to ever attract another partner.
11. I fear that I can never be happy on my own.
12. I fear that I can never be happy with another person.
13. I fear that I can never have a partner who fulfills me.
14. I fear that I can never have a life as an individual if I am also in a relationship.
15. I fear that the damage from my childhood can never be repaired.
16. I fear that I can never duplicate my parents' loving marriage.

17. I fear that I am destined to duplicate my parents' dysfunctional marriage.

18. I fear that my anger will always get the best of me and destroy my relationships.

19. I fear being emotionally out of control.

20. I fear being hurt again.

21. I fear _____.

22. I fear _____.

23. I fear _____.

24. I fear _____.

25. I fear _____.

Managing Fear in Order to Move Forward

Now that you have defined your fears on paper, you need to find ways of managing them. Fears are a normal part of life. They are not insurmountable. In fact, in many areas of your life, you are probably able to control your fears successfully by seeing them as challenges to be overcome. Consider your work life. If a problem is presented to you by a client, employee, or a colleague, does it make you panic or are you able to manage the situation on your own? Rather than relying on your boss to tell you what to do, you, like most people, are probably able to assess the situation and find a solution on your own. Because we see our work persona in a different light than our personal persona, we go about handling fears in a different way with colleagues and clients than in our private lives. But those same muscles you flex in other areas of your life can be applied to your situation as a newly divorced person.

Exercise 2: Recognizing Your Competencies

In this exercise, think of three areas in your life where you feel competent and in charge. They may be situations at work, as a parent, in managing your money, in managing your health, or in taking care of your home. Describe how you feel when you accomplish tasks that make you feel in control, using adjectives you could apply to other areas of your life.

The next time you are feeling vulnerable or frightened, consider these situations again. Embrace your accomplishments and let that feeling give you strength.

Exercise 3: Embracing Your Fears; Embracing Yourself

Relationships are the places in our lives that make us most vulnerable, so it's only natural to feel a sense of panic when you lose a partner. Like the toddler who feels the world is safe and friendly until his mother turns out the light and leaves him alone to face the boogeyman, you may feel a sense of terror in the face of divorce. After the breakup of my marriage, I did. I'd lie awake nights worrying about being alone, making enough money to support myself and my daughters, parenting my children by myself, or getting over my pain enough to ever consider another relationship. In the past when I faced a challenge, my reaction was to call my husband, Michael, and ask for his advice or support. With the divorce, that option had changed dramatically.

So I decided I would make my fears my friends. This is how I'd walk myself through it. I'd say, "Okay, this feeling of panic has come up again, so instead of rejecting it or running from it, I'm going to face it. What is it I am afraid of? What do I need to do to overcome that?" Visualizing my fear and a positive outcome was also helpful: I'd imagine myself standing on a surfboard riding a wave that I knew would peak and gradually end.

In this next exercise, I'd like you to do the same. Let's start with the big waves: Returning to the list from Exercise 1, write down the top five things you fear most.

Now, following my example above, identify for yourself what you are afraid of in each of these scenarios. Think of how you can overcome that fear. Do you need help from a professional to manage your money? Would spending time with friends and family more often give you the support you need to feel lovable? Could a parenting class provide you with the confidence you need to face life as a single parent? The exercises below will give you additional tools and techniques for understanding and managing your fears.

What you should not do is try to control your fears by ignoring them or cutting yourself off from others. The tendency when worry and panic set in is to either super-busy yourself or isolate yourself to avoid the fear and pain. Instead, you need to use fear as a motivator and find coping skills to help you overcome it—not by ignoring your fears or being consumed by them, but by coming up with solutions. A therapist can be very helpful in this process, something I will address in Chapter 8.

Every time you embrace a fear and conquer it, your "I" becomes stronger and you are better able to handle the next challenge. Soon, that approach becomes a way of life, just as your competence at your job or elsewhere is second nature. Handling things on your own doesn't mean you can't share the problem with others, including your ex-spouse or a friend or relative, but just like presenting a problem and its resolution to a boss, showing your strength mentally and emotionally to yourself in your personal life gives you a great sense of accomplishment. So before automatically turning to someone else for advice, first check in with yourself. You may be surprised at how resourceful you are if you give yourself the chance. As Eleanor Roosevelt once said, "Do one thing every day that scares you." Facing your fears is the path to greater strength.

"Every time you embrace a fear and conquer it, your 'I' becomes stronger and you are better able to handle the next challenge."

Childhood Fears and the Roots of Defensive Behaviors

Just as you are feeling a rush of emotions in response to the end of your marriage, when you were a child you probably felt pain, fear, anger, or shame in response to certain parenting behaviors. Feeling vulnerable and out of control after divorce, when it can seem that you don't have control over your own destiny, is actually quite similar. But there is one big difference: your ability as an adult to manage your feelings and work through them in constructive ways.

As a child, because you were still developing psychologically, emotionally, and physically, may not have felt secure enough in your primary attachment, and lacked other models for behavior, you were unable to express your feelings directly. Your way of managing them was to develop distorted ways of expressing yourself, with various maladaptive behaviors. Those behaviors became such an ingrained response to feeling helpless, that you likely still use some of them today. As an adult, you have many other options and pathways for constructively and effectively managing situations and relationships. In order to move forward and change, you must access those childhood feelings you previously defended against so you can more effectively handle the dysfunctional aspects of your current behavior, particularly those that negatively impacted your marriage.

"It takes time and energy to look at your past, evaluate it, and move toward change. As ambitious and eager as you might be to transform yourself, you can't just open that door and run through it."

You are probably asking yourself how in the world you can gain access to those deeply buried feelings. Although this task may seem daunting, in the section on defenses that follows we will look at the method by which you can reconstruct those early feelings. Identifying your defense mechanisms and dysfunctional behavior helps you reconstruct the past and allows you to gain access to the feelings you defend against.

During this process, keep in mind that it takes time and energy to look at your past, evaluate it, and move toward change. As ambitious and eager as you might be to transform yourself, you can't just open that door and run through it. There is no magic moment. Especially in its early stages, change is a process that encompasses fear and resistance. That ambivalence is understandable and in fact normal, because change brings about uncertainty and threatens your security and your very identity. In the end, many people fail to change for one simple reason: a familiar Self can be more reassuring than a new Self.

The Steps That Make Up Change

The data give you an idea of what to expect as you begin this journey. Through years of research, change experts James Prochaska, John Norcross, and Carlo DiClemente have discovered that change takes place in stages over a long period of time and that it rarely occurs in a neat linear fashion. In fact, they claim that when it comes to solving problems, "Relapse is the rule rather than the exception." In their book *Changing for Good*, they define the stages of change as precontemplation, contemplation, preparation, action, maintenance, and termination. Because you have been motivated by the trauma of divorce to pick up this book, you are most likely in the contemplation stage: aware you have a problem, struggling to understand its causes, and trying to find a solution.

In order to work through that resistance and not get stuck in the contemplation stage, as many people do, you need to become conscious of the defense mechanisms that you have used all your life as you prepare for action. The function of these defenses, which developed in childhood, was to protect your conscious Self from being overwhelmed by feelings it could not manage. Not surprisingly, these same defenses were in play during your marriage, keeping you in the dark about your contribution to the interpersonal problems you experienced as part of a couple. In both cases, it's only when these defenses come down and knowledge about yourself increases that you are in a position to move forward into action.

"You need to become conscious of the defense mechanisms that you have used all your life as you prepare for action. The function of these defenses, which developed in childhood, was to protect your conscious Self from being overwhelmed by feelings it could not manage."

Defense Mechanisms

From an evolutionary standpoint, defensive behavior actually makes a lot of sense: these mechanisms are coping strategies that protect us from being aware of thoughts or feelings we cannot tolerate. They shield us from harm, either physically or emotionally. Further, they are unconscious reactions, allowing us to sufficiently distance ourselves from uncomfortable feelings or thoughts instinctively. That all seems good, right?

But defense mechanisms have their dark side, too. They can rob us of the positive aspects of our emotions. They inhibit spontaneity, reduce our flexibility to respond to change, and interfere with our ability to connect with others.

To get an idea of this, let's take a look at how defense mechanisms develop. The defenses each of us uses—and there are many—come in large part from the mother-child bond. Just as our caregiver taught us how to interact with others, she also taught us how to defend ourselves from others through example. When we watched our caregiver deal with stress, we unconsciously absorbed that behavior and adopted it when we ourselves felt stressed—even when the person stressing us was the caregiver herself. So, for example, if an infant desires to be held by its mother and the mother is unavailable, the child learns that it is better not to feel those needs. In essence, he or she is learning to defend against the need for affection. These early defenses are adaptive, because they enable an infant to preserve emotional connection with the caregiver—even if it's in an unhealthy way. That connection is paramount; infants and children can't survive without it.

Adults can't survive without emotional connection either. But unlike infants, they don't need to resort to unhealthy behaviors in order to do it, and they also have the capacity to interact in a more sophisticated way, unlike their internal child counterpart did. Yet those simpler defenses are where we all begin, so let's start by taking a look at some of the defenses rooted in the developmental process and how they play out in adulthood.

Primitive Defenses

Since defenses are learned early, when the nervous system is still developing, they can be hard to recognize by the time you become an adult—they just feel like a natural part of you. For that same reason, defenses are not easy to let go, even once you've identified them. But identifying your defenses is the first step toward changing them. Following the progression of change outlined by Prochaska, Norcross, and DiClemente, people defend against change in the precontemplation stage; once they recognize there is a problem and begin to plan how they will react to it, they have moved into contemplation, and defenses begin to come down.

Psychologists have categorized defense mechanisms based on how primitive they are. The more primitive the mechanism, the less effectively it will work over time. Here are the most foundational mechanisms we use, from early childhood on. As you will see in the examples I give for adults, these are usually not the most effective approaches when interacting with a spouse.

Denial – Denial is the refusal to accept reality or fact, instead acting as though a painful event, thought, or feeling does not exist. A child, when caught doing something she knows is wrong, may say, "I didn't pinch the baby"—even though it's clear she did. Similarly, an adult may reject his anger in response to humiliating criticism by saying, "I'm not angry with my wife."

Regression – Regression is when you revert to an earlier stage of development, usually immature behavior, in order to avoid

110

unacceptable thoughts and feelings. A child may, for example, suck his thumb or try to crawl into his mother's lap when she is angry at him, even though he is too big for that behavior. An adult may regress by refusing to get out of bed and engage in daily activities when faced with a spouse's disapproval.

Acting Out – Acting out is behaving in an extreme manner in order to express thoughts or feelings a person feels incapable of expressing otherwise. A child may lie on the grocery store floor kicking and screaming when she is told she can't have candy. An adult might throw a book at his wife or put his fist through the wall rather than saying, "I am angry with you" to his spouse.

Projection – Projection is the misattribution of a person's undesired thoughts, feelings, or impulses onto another person. A child, when acting grumpy and difficult, might say, "It's Suzie's fault. She hit me first." The adult counterpart might snap, "Don't tell me I'm being unreasonable. Why do you hate me?"

Reaction Formation – Reaction formation is converting unwanted or dangerous thoughts, feelings, or impulses into their opposites. A firstborn child, jealous of a new sibling, may show his anger by aggressively "hugging" the baby, for example. An adult, complaining about how critical her husband is of her, may suddenly shift gears and say, "Really, he's a great guy."

More-Mature Defense Mechanisms

Primitive defense mechanisms come naturally to most people. As mentioned earlier, they also lose their efficacy when used by adults. Oftentimes, more-mature mechanisms take their place—defenses children see used between their parents or in other adults and older children. Though more sophisticated, they, too, are less-than-ideal ways of dealing with one's feelings and thoughts. You will likely identify with a few of these behaviors as well.

Displacement – Displacement is redirecting the thoughts, feelings, or impulses you have toward one person to another person. People often use displacement when they cannot express their feelings in a safe manner to the person they are meant for. So a husband who is feeling angry at and humiliated by his boss for something that happened at work may come home and yell at his wife or push her away. He may even voice his displacement and confusion by saying something like, "I'm so furious at my partner, and I don't even know why!"

Rationalization – Rationalization is defined as creating false but plausible excuses to justify unacceptable feelings, behaviors, or impulses. A married man may flirt with other women, for example, and rationalize it by saying, "My wife is bored with me, and this isn't really cheating, so what does a little flirting hurt?"

Intellectualization – Intellectualization is an overemphasis on thinking when confronted with an unacceptable feeling or impulse. It's a type of rationalization, only more cerebral, which helps create greater distance from the emotion at hand. For example, a woman who's accused of spending too much money on frivolous items by her husband may counter that she has researched and applied for credit cards with the lowest interest rates, keeps track of the amount she's saving by buying things on sale, and buys in bulk in order to save more money per item.

Undoing – Undoing is an attempt to take back a behavior or emotion that is unacceptable. One tries to undo behavior or expressed emotions by doing something that indicates the opposite. So a husband who has criticized his wife may try to undo her anger by buying her flowers or taking her out to dinner.

What Defenses Do You Use?

Just as everyone's development is unique, so are the defenses each of us uses. In order to evaluate and address our defenses, first we need to identify them clearly. The goal of this next exercise is to continue becoming more honest with your inner and real Self. It's important to reflect on these questions, feel them, and own them as completely as possible.

Exercise 4: This Is How I Operate

Complete the following as honestly and spontaneously as you can.

1. When I don't get what I want I ...
2. I find the best way to get things done is to ...

3. Phrases I always use during a fight are ...
4. I try to smooth things over by ...
5. The way I make things up to others is to ...
6. The mask I sometimes wear is ...
7. On the surface people see me as ...
8. The game I played in my marriage was to ...
9. The real me hides under ...
10. Most people don't know that I ...

Triggers

Defenses don't just rise up out of the blue. Whether we are consciously aware of it or not, each of us has triggers that set off our defensive behaviors. These, too, may be deeply ingrained from what we experienced in childhood. For example, you may have watched your mother acting very deferential and accommodating of your dad, but rather than placating him, her lack of assertiveness always caused your father to explode in anger and start a fight. As you grew older, you, too, may have been frustrated and angered when your mother tried to appease you with codependent behavior. Following your father's lead, you may have started blowing up at her when she did this. That trigger, the lack of assertion in others, would eventually cause you to lash out at people you are close to (such as your spouse) when they exhibited this behavior.

What you may not have realized is that your mother was showing her own triggered defense. She may have been afraid of her father and his quick temper and displaced that fear onto her husband, using the same coping mechanism to try to calm him down as she (or her mother) used on her father.

In this next exercise, let's take a look at specific situations in your marriage and the triggers that caused your defenses to click in. Then we'll compare what provoked you and the defenses you used to alienate yourself from your true feelings to childhood experiences you had or witnessed with your primary caregivers.

Exercise 5: You Make Me So Crazy!

1. Begin by listing three things you and your spouse argued about. The following scenarios may be helpful in triggering your memory:

   - I come home from a long day at work and the house is a mess, dinner isn't ready, and my spouse, who's been home for a while, is watching TV.

   - I open the credit card bill and see a huge list of charges for things we can't afford.

   - I want to have sex, but my partner is unresponsive.

   - My spouse was the last one to use the car, and the gas tank is empty.

   - He/she promised to have some alone time with me tonight, but is working late—again.

   - While I was out running errands, he/she allowed the kids to play video games for hours and eat a bunch of junk food, even though we talked about restricting their computer time and feeding them a healthy diet.

2. Now think about what you typically say or do when these situations arise. Here are some typical responses:

   – Ignore it. It will only make things worse if you start an argument. (Denial)

   – Start to whine or plead with baby talk. (Regression)

   – Yell, throw something, or go to your room and slam the door. (Acting out)

   – Say, "Why do you do these things? Is it because you don't love me anymore?" (Projection)

   – Start dinner/get out the checkbook/drive the car to the gas station/etc. Say, in a clipped tone, "It's fine. I'll do it." (Reaction formation)

   – Yell at the kids. (Displacement)

   – Start an argument, then offer to take your spouse to dinner so you can kiss and make up. (Undoing)

3. You've just pinpointed some of your triggers and the defenses you use to hide your true feelings. Now it's time to think about similar situations you witnessed in your primary family. Many people hear their mother or father's words coming out of their mouth when they fight with their spouses. If you do, what did they say? What did they tend to argue about? How did their fights play out? What were the defenses you saw them using? (It can be useful to think in terms of codependent and counter-dependent

116

behaviors, as outlined in Chapter 5.) How have
you integrated those same responses into
your own adult life?

Consciousness-Raising

In the last two exercises, you were engaging in a therapeutic
process known as "consciousness-raising." Becoming aware of
how you manage your innermost thoughts and feelings is a
necessary and vital step during the contemplation stage. Your
objective is to develop a greater awareness of your defense
mechanisms, where they came from, and how they contributed
to destructive behaviors in your marriage. Once you are well-
informed about your habitual behaviors and their consequences,
the next step in your journey is to question whether you can
have positive interactions with others while continuing with
those behaviors.

*"Once you are well-informed about your habitual behaviors
and their consequences, the next step in your journey is to
question whether you can have positive interactions
with others while continuing with those behaviors."*

The following is a brief self-assessment that will help you
gauge whether moving forward with your old defenses makes
sense or if you need to find a better way to manage relationships
and their stressors. Please be honest and realistic in your answers.

Exercise 6: Is This Behavior Working?

1. Replay one of the scenarios from the last exercise, step 1, in your mind. Pretend as though you are an audience member in a movie theatre watching a film and be as emotionally neutral as possible. Focusing only on your own behavior, how do you feel about the way you managed stress in that particular situation? Did your methods work? Did you end the experience feeling happy, calm, and with your needs met? If not, what feelings did you feel? Were those negative feelings familiar?

2. Now think of the same scenario, only this time, explore different ways you could have reacted to the trigger. See yourself talking the situation through with your spouse rationally and expressing how the situation made you feel. Write down how your interaction in the conversation could have gone if you avoided your usual defense mechanisms. What do you think would have been the result?

3. Compare the two scenarios. If you continue using your usual defenses, what will be the cost to you? Reflect on the costs of your interactions with your spouse in the past. Did they hurt your self-image, sap your energy, increase your stress levels, or make you feel depressed, sad, or angry? If any of the following is true, consider what it would feel like not to have the burden of those feelings when you interact with a person you love.

4. Make a list of pros and cons to leaving your defense mechanisms behind. How would that affect your health, your time, your sense of yourself and your spouse? If those arguments ended differently, what would you do with the time you formerly spent feeling mad, frustrated, manipulated, or unheard?

Preparing to Take Action

According to Prochaska, Norcross, and DiClemente, the preparation stage is the cornerstone of effective action. It is at this juncture that you make a solid commitment to behavior change—even though you are not yet ready to act—and this will increase your likelihood of success.

Any residual resistance to change must be resolved during this stage. In the preparation stage, you will continue to reevaluate yourself and your behaviors and feel increasingly confident about your desire to change. During this time you will find yourself thinking more about your future Self and the hopeful vision of what life will be like and less about your problematic past and the pain it has caused you.

Moving through the phases of change, just like moving through the phases of grief, is not a linear process. You will find yourself reverting back to deeply ingrained defensive behaviors, reacting to triggers, and debating whether you are up to the challenges of change. The series of questions can help you check in with yourself when you find yourself circling back to those old familiar reactions.

Exercise 7: Checking In with Yourself

When you find yourself reacting to stress with your old defense style, ask yourself the following questions and try the following exercises:

1. Ask yourself, "Do I have the choice to change my behavior in this situation?"

2. Stop whatever you are doing and breathe deeply. Count to ten.

3. Tell the person who is pushing your buttons how that makes you feel. Be as calm and honest as you can. Or, consider that this may not be a situation to express your feelings, but rather one to contain them and work through them internally.

4. Think about the willpower you have shown you have in other areas of your life (review Exercise 2, "Recognizing Your Competencies"). Encourage yourself that you can do this.

5. Envision yourself as you want to be: happy, confident, calm, mature, complete.

6. Discuss how this situation can be resolved so it doesn't keep happening. Come up with actionable steps to resolving this problem.

As the last step in the previous exercise emphasizes, now that you are relinquishing your old behaviors, you will need to substitute healthy responses for the old patterns you have developed. By exploring what both destructive and good, functional interdependency between partners looks like in Chapter 7, we will take a look at some possible substitutes.

Chapter 7

Characteristics of Healthy Intimacy: How to Remain Separate but Connected

The primary focus of my counseling is first and foremost to help my patients define the Self they have been protecting behind their many defenses. Who is the person beneath those compensatory behaviors? What are their feelings, thoughts, needs, wants, hopes, and dreams? Post-divorce, my patients are given a second chance to define their "I" and make themselves whole. Through their own motivations, they put themselves in charge of their lives. A major step along the way is learning to establish healthy boundaries and thereby, paradoxically, enhance the opportunity for true intimacy.

"A healthy relationship cannot exist until each person has clearly defined personal boundaries. All relationships are made up of three distinct entities: two individuals and the life they share between them."

It Takes Three to Make a Relationship

A healthy relationship cannot exist until each person has clearly defined personal boundaries. All relationships are made up of three distinct entities: two individuals and the life they share between them. The individuals must be whole and autonomous, and have a unique identity separate from the relationship. Each participant must also grant his or her partner the right to have their own feelings, thoughts, needs, and viewpoints, which will be different from their own. To nourish the third entity, the relationship, individuals need to be able to express themselves and reveal their inner lives while also being sensitive to how they affect their partner and how their partner affects them.

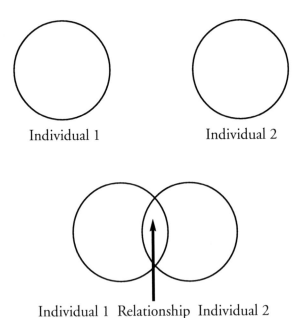

Individual 1   Individual 2

Individual 1 Relationship Individual 2

124

The paradox of being separate and connected, that one plus one does not equal either one (two merged individuals) or two (two individuals with little intimacy between them) but three (two individuals and their relationship), flies in the face of what we have been taught about romantic relationships. As Dennis Bagarozzi says in his book *Enhancing Intimacy in Marriage*, "A truly romantic idea in heterosexual love is the belief that total union in all areas of intimacy with a person of the opposite sex completes the self." In contrast, he says "mature love," his term for a relationship that involves two people who are not enmeshed or merged, "can develop only between two individuals who have successfully separated and individuated from their primary caretakers and families of origin, have solidified a positive identity, and have developed a fully integrated self." He goes on to say, "The cornerstone of a mature love relationship is a free and willing commitment to the other person as well as a commitment to the growth and the development of the relationship as a whole." In other words, it takes three to tango.

"What makes mature love possible are healthy boundaries, knowing what is yours, respecting what is not, and avoiding transferring or imposing your feelings, desires, and viewpoints onto your partner."

What makes mature love possible are healthy boundaries, knowing what is yours, respecting what is not, and avoiding transferring or imposing your feelings, desires, and viewpoints onto your partner.

Charles Whitfield, in his book *Boundaries and Relationships: Knowing, Protecting, and Enjoying the Self*, provides a very clear picture of what belongs to the Self and how that is separate from what belongs to others:

What Is Mine

1. My awareness of my inner life

2. My inner life, including: my beliefs, thoughts, feelings, decisions, choices, experiences, wants and needs

3. My behavior

4. The responsibility to make my life successful and joyful

---------------------- Healthy Boundaries----------------------

What Is Not Mine

1. Others' awareness of their inner life

2. Material from others' inner life, including: their beliefs, thoughts, feelings, decisions, choices, experiences, wants and needs

3. Their behavior

4. The responsibility to make their life successful and joyful

As a chart, it all looks very simple. In practice, being aware of what is yours and what is not can get murky quickly. One of the problems is the idealization that characterizes the symbiotic phase of the developmental process, in both the mother-infant bond and adult romantic relationships. You will remember that the first stage in the development of Self, symbiosis, is characterized by all-consuming love. Like the early symbiotic attachments between mother and child, the nature of the adult romantic bond is also intense and merged. When we start out in symbiosis as parents or lovers, one of the ways we define the other person, whether it is a child or a partner, is through the fantasies we create about them in addition to the actual cues they give us. We want to see in the people we love a reflection of ourselves: similar views of the world, likes and dislikes, hopes and dreams. In this enmeshed state, individuals typically regard one another as long-sought soul mates who truly understand one another. In addition to seeing the world as we do, we also want our adult partners to repair our wounds, even spare us the burden of growing up. That need to idealize and protect is encouraged culturally in the *Jerry Maguire*-style "you complete me" ideals we see in the media. For all these reasons, many people think symbiosis, one plus one equals one, is how a relationship should be.

But each individual in the couple has progressed through his or her own separation-individuation process and brings an idiosyncratic history of managing closeness and distance, complex emotions, aggression, disillusionment, competition, and ambivalence into their adult relationships. In cases where the developmental process in childhood was inhibited by anxious

127

or aloof parenting, codependent or counter-dependent behaviors are included in the mix, and boundaries become even more fuzzy. Children who were enmeshed with parents who didn't allow them to individuate become adults who have a hard time defining Self without being unduly dependent on the influences of others. Kids who were left to fend for themselves during the crucial differentiation and rapprochement stages have a very rigid sense of separation from others that doesn't allow for the trust, acceptance, and respect needed to form a healthy relationship.

Boundaries and Defenses

Boundaries and defenses, which we discussed in Chapter 6, arise both in childhood and adult relationships when we feel our needs are not being met as we expect them to be. The defenses we use can function in constructive ways to define what is ours and what is not, or in unintentionally unhealthy ways to blur the distinction between the Self and the Other. Consider this example. A patient of mine, Anne, was married to Richie, who often found himself behaving in childlike ways (regression) when they argued. If Richie felt his opinions were not being heard or he was not seeing the outcome he wanted, he would begin to whine, tell Anne she wasn't being fair, and continue with this childish behavior until he got his way. Richie's mother was extremely codependent and used the same technique as her fighting style. Through modeling, she taught her son to resolve conflict by resorting to immature behavior. By using this manipulative technique, Richie was making Anne responsible for his needs, as if he were a child and she his caregiver. If Richie had successfully individuated as a child, he would have been equipped to see himself and Anne as two separate but equal individuals with different needs that could be discussed and even disagreed about calmly, without blame, and without a forced "winner" and "loser."

Another patient, Sam, used a different defense mechanism, projection, which also served to undermine the differentiation between him and his wife. Sam had been abandoned as a child but had gone on to become a successful businessman. He had a domineering personality, though inside he still felt very vulnerable about being cast aside by his parents. One of the ways he expressed this counter-dependency was to continuously insist that his wife, Ellen, participate in his many hobbies, though he was never interested in doing the things she enjoyed. On one occasion in particular, Sam booked a two-week vacation to Belgium for the two of them without consulting Ellen. He wanted to tour a dozen Belgian breweries so he could taste all his favorite beers. Ellen had no interest in beer and would much rather have spent their vacation in Italy, exploring art museums. When Ellen suggested a different itinerary that incorporated both Belgium and Italy, Sam's reply was "Why are you fighting me on this—do you have any idea how hard I work so we can have a nice life? You're just like my parents; you just don't care about me."

Sam created a very rigid boundary with his wife by imposing a "you're either with me or against me" stance. Though using a very different technique and coming from a very different background, Sam, just like Richie, could not separate "what is mine" from "what is not mine" and see his spouse as an individual whose opinions, experiences, wants, and needs should be considered and honored with empathy and respect.

"How many times in your previous marriage did you think or say to your spouse that if only he/she would see things your way and make a few alterations to his/her behavior, everything would be all right? ... This controlling and self-focused behavior is the antithesis of the collaboration we should aim for."

Where Do I Draw the Line?

If we think about them at all, most of us tend to think that our defense mechanisms protect us from pain and hurt. Yet when we take a closer look at them, as we did in Chapter 6 and in the previous examples, we see how ineffectual defense mechanisms can actually be. They often don't protect but instead undermine the important differences that exist between us and the ones we love. How many times in your previous marriage did you think or say to your spouse that if only he/she would see things your way and make a few alterations to his/her behavior, everything would be all right—just as Richie and Sam were doing? This controlling and self-focused behavior is the antithesis of the collaboration we should aim for.

Examining our defenses and adjusting our personal boundaries can offer a closer connection to others. "Setting healthy boundaries and limits is a way to deal with and prevent unnecessary pain and suffering," says Charles Whitfield in *Boundaries and Relationships*. "If any time during this relationship I do not maintain this healthy openness and balance, I may become addicted, attached or compulsive about the relationship"—or controlling, manipulative, and detached.

The first step toward establishing more healthy boundaries is to understand where the boundaries were in your marriage and if they were healthy or unhealthy.

Exercise 1: Is This Mine?

In this first exercise, we will explore boundaries in your previous marriage and how you felt about them by examining things you commonly did with your ex-spouse.

First, write down five activities you and your husband or wife shared often. They can be anything from playing a sport together to traveling to a particular destination to choosing how you would decorate your home to having sex or watching TV.

For each activity, ask yourself the following questions:

1. Did you choose the activity together or was one partner responsible for the choice?

2. Did one partner always initiate the activity or have control over it?

3. Did either of you ever feel you did not have the option of saying no to the activity?

4. Even if you or your spouse knew you could refuse to participate, did either of you frequently say yes just to keep from rocking the boat?

5. If you argued about the activity, did the result of those arguments vary, or was there a clear "winner"?

6. Did the activity make you feel closer as a couple?

Thinking about how you interacted in these activities can provide a snapshot of the kinds of boundaries that existed in your marriage. If you commonly went along with things your spouse chose when you didn't really want to, you exhibited a tendency toward fused boundaries by allowing him or her to force their worldview on you. If you nearly always set the agenda and ignored your spouse on the occasions they protested or told them, "You'll love this" or "This will be good for you," you exhibited a tendency toward maintaining rigid boundaries. In either case, the opportunity for true intimacy was missing. If, however, you chose the activity together, resolved any conflicts you may have had about it, looked forward to it and talked about it frequently, it was an area in your life where you achieved intimacy that could have been extended to other parts of your marriage—and can be in future relationships.

"Understanding the various ways you experience intimacy and what is most important to you will enable you to strengthen that third component of a relationship, the relationship itself, in future relationships, as well as honoring the strengths and differences of the two people involved."

What Is Intimacy?

In the opening chapter of his book *Enhancing Intimacy in Marriage*, Dennis Bagarozzi defines intimacy in this way: "Central to [intimacy] is knowledge, understanding, and acceptance of the other, as well as empathy for the other person's feelings and an appreciation for his or her unique view of the world."

Bagarozzi's definition points to the fact that intimacy is a way of relating to others in more ways than just sexual. In fact, Bagarozzi divides intimacy into nine components: emotional, psychological, intellectual, sexual, physical but not sexual, spiritual, aesthetic, social/recreational, and temporal. Different people have different levels of need for each component. Some people may require lots of physical connection with their partner in the form of hugs, snuggling, kissing, and non-sexual touching. Others may feel the need to relate with their spouse emotionally by sharing their feelings or aesthetically by experiencing and discussing art, literature, or music. Individuals may desire a great deal of sexual intimacy, intellectual stimulation, or shared social and recreational activities. It all depends on the person.

Understanding the various ways you experience intimacy and what is most important to you will enable you to strengthen that third component of a relationship, the relationship itself, in future relationships, as well as honoring the strengths and differences of the two people involved.

Exercise 2: Intimacy Is a Many-Faceted Thing

In the last exercise, in addition to exploring boundaries, you also unknowingly explored how you and your former spouse felt about the different components of intimacy. You may have considered activities that are recreational, aesthetic, sexual, or intellectual when you came up with the list of things you did together. If a particular activity was one you both enjoyed, you and your partner had a similar "needs level" for that kind of intimacy. If it was forced upon you or by you, a discrepancy existed regarding your shared desire for that kind of intimacy, and unhealthy boundaries may have attempted to force a more equal needs level.

This next exercise will help establish which components of intimacy are important to you.

Exercise 3: My Intimacy Needs

1. Make a list of the top ten to twenty things that bring you joy. These may be things you do alone, with a romantic partner, or with friends or family. To qualify these activities, look for those things that make you feel complete, alleviate worry and stress, make you feel loved, at one with yourself and the world, and content.

2. Considering Bagarozzi's components of intimacy, organize your list according to whether the activities are emotional, psychological, intellectual, sexual, physical but not sexual, spiritual, aesthetic, social/recreational, and temporal. Some definitions will help:[2]

   a. Emotional intimacy is communicating feelings, both positive and negative, freely.

   b. Psychological intimacy is sharing hopes, dreams, worries, and other deeply held beliefs without fear of being judged.

---

[2] Summarized from Bagarozzi, *Enhancing Intimacy in Marriage.*

c. Intellectual intimacy is discussing ideas in an open, stimulating exchange. It is important not to confuse intellectual intimacy with the defense mechanism of intellectualization (see Chapter 6).

d. Sexual intimacy can include watching erotic movies, reading sexually explicit poetry, dancing suggestively, etc. in addition to having sex.

e. Physical intimacy includes cuddling, hugging, holding hands, etc.

f. Spiritual intimacy is sharing one's spiritual beliefs with another. Though religious beliefs fall into this category, spiritual beliefs do not have to be tied to a particular orthodoxy.

g. Aesthetic intimacy includes looking at and discussing art, attending plays or concerts, watching the sun set together, etc.

h. Social and recreational intimacy includes engaging in sports, sharing hobbies, enjoying meals together, travelling, or just talking about everyday matters over coffee.

i. Temporal intimacy is the amount of time you want to share with your partner in any of these activities overall. Are you someone who can connect in an hour each day, or would you like to spend large chunks of time with your partner consistently?

3. You now have an idea of which components of intimacy are most important to you. How does this

compare with your impression of what was important to your ex-spouse? If your intimacy needs differed, were you able to fulfill those needs with other people in your life, for example by travelling with a sibling or parent, going to movies and concerts with a friend, or playing tennis with your tennis group? Was that interaction enough, or did you need that sense of closeness with your spouse as well? For many, certain intimacy needs can be met outside a relationship, while others must be met within it. Keep in mind that a romantic relationship is meant to honor the differences between the participants as well as their similarities. Your partner is not there to complete you and be responsible for your happiness—that is your job.

Honoring Your Similarities as Well as Your Differences

Identifying your intimacy needs, seeing how they align with a partner's, and finding a comfortable space where you share the many facets of intimacy is a crucial step in finding that place where two "I's" become a "we." Before embarking on a new relationship, you should have a clear sense of what your intimacy needs are, what's important to you in a relationship, and what needs—intellectual, emotional, aesthetic, spiritual, etc.—you can happily fulfill outside the relationship, with friends, family, or on your own. In examining intimacy needs as a whole, you need to ask yourself, "What am I looking to a partner to do for me that I can do for myself?"

You also need to ask yourself what intimate experiences you

can share with your partner, knowing what is important to him or her emotionally, intellectually, spiritually, psychologically, and so on—and honoring how those needs are different from your own. James Hollis says it beautifully in his book *Finding Meaning in the Second Half of Life: How to Finally, Really Grow Up*:

> What another really can bring to us, their greatest gift, is not an imitation or confirmation of our limited vision, but the gift of their quite different vision, their otherness as otherness. The immature psyche needs confirmation to be secure, a cloning of interests and sensibilities, and there is no surer path to staying immature and undeveloped than seeking agreement in all things. …
>
> A more mature relationship is based on "otherness" itself, on the dialectical principle that demonstrates that my one and your one together create the third … We do not learn and grow by all subscribing to the same school of thought, copying the same values or voting the same way. We grow from the experience of our differences, although in insecure moments we quickly forget this.

"What another really can bring to us, their greatest gift, is not an imitation or confirmation of our limited vision, but the gift of their quite different vision, their otherness as otherness." — James Hollis

---

This sort of growth and respect takes a very conscious and concerted effort. As the previous intimacy exercises may have shown you, post-symbiosis we begin to recognize more clearly that our partners don't have the same needs and worldview as we do. Defining those differences honestly and respecting them is challenging. In fact, more than likely during your marriage you and your partner mismanaged some of your differences. Instead of embracing them to enhance the relationship, they probably became a source of stress and distance between you.

Seeing differences as negatives, and even exploiting them with aversive conflict-resolution strategies as Richie and Sam did in the previous examples, often stems from having been shamed, humiliated, or even threatened by your primary caregiver when you showed your intimacy needs as a child. As an adult, when you found yourself in situations with your partner where differences needed to be recognized and worked out, you may have instead resorted to the ineffective, controlling, and painful strategies you experienced and/or developed earlier in life. Let's look at an example for how this can play out and what can been done to honor differences.

Mishandling Differences: A Case Study

Ken and his partner, Judy, are getting dressed for a night out to the theater with some friends. All day Judy has been thinking about how much she loves the theater and how excited she is about this performance. It has always been important to Judy that Ken likes the arts too, and Ken knows this.

Eagerly anticipating the evening, when Ken arrives home from work to shower and change, Judy asks excitedly, "Aren't you looking forward to tonight?" Instead of agreeing with Judy, though, Ken responds by saying, "You know how I hate sitting through depressing plays. I really wish we were doing something else." Judy responds by raising her voice and saying, "It is always about you. No matter what I want to do, you disagree. You have a way of ruining my excitement about the things I love most." Ken replies in frustration, "You asked for my opinion. I gave it to you and now you're angry that I told you the truth. I can't win. You're so sensitive about these things, Judy. Okay, then, I'm excited about the play. Can we just have a nice evening out?" Judy turns to have Ken zip up her dress then gives him a peck on the cheek as a way of thanking him for his submission.

Although Judy and Ken do not generally have serious arguments, this scene is typical and repetitious of the dance they do and the ways they attack each other when differences come up. Is Ken wrong for voicing his opinion about the play when Judy asked for it? Is Judy wrong for being so sensitive to Ken's honesty? Has the conflict between them been adequately resolved?

Let's look more closely at Judy and Ken's argument and think about how it fits into the relationship model of two "I's" and a "we," as well as how influences from Judy and Ken's childhood individuation play into the way they responded to a difference between them.

In this particular instance, Judy is especially sensitive to Ken's views about the theater. If Judy's intimacy needs were assessed, her need for aesthetic intimacy would show itself as being very high. As a teenager, Judy fell in love with drama, to her mother's dismay. Her mom continuously criticized Judy for something she thought was frivolous, and she refused to pay for Judy's college tuition if she studied theater. Consequently, Judy developed a reliance on Ken's professed love for artistic activities—going to art galleries, seeing serious films, attending the theater. Although she requested his opinion and he likely meant no harm to her by being honest about how certain plays made him feel, she clearly heard it as a criticism (projection) and overreacted by attacking him. In fact, Judy's response to Ken was intense enough that it appears she may have confused legitimate disagreement as disapproval.

Ken, on the other hand, was the youngest of three boys and was continuously compared to his older brothers. For that reason, he developed a high need for emotional intimacy: feeling loved and accepted by his parents, and of equal value in their eyes to his brothers. When those emotional needs were not met, Ken developed a view of himself as always coming up short, and so he often said or did things he didn't really want to do (reaction formation). So when Judy retaliated by saying Ken never says anything right, she zeroed right in on Ken's hot button—not living up to Judy's expectations of him—which Ken found hurtful, and so he complied with her wishes despite his own.

Who's responsible for the conflict between them? In truth, they both are. The exchange between Judy and Ken is defined by an overreaction of their "I's" and unhealthy defense mechanisms—projection and reaction formation. Neither honored their differences; in fact Ken was coerced into going to the play.

Although Judy got what she wanted, and there seemed to be a semblance of peace between them, their "we" didn't benefit from this form of conflict resolution. Although this was not a serious issue, we can imagine that enough repetitions of this negative dance will create serious alienation between Judy and Ken.

Different "I's"; A Compatible "We"

Partners need to experience security with one another so they can express themselves honestly and bring their "I's" into the partnership openly. It's not unlike the infant who needs the reassurance of a safe "home base" (the primary caregiver) to express his or her developing identity. When that sense of security is there, sympathy and empathy result—for the child as well as for the adult. And sympathy and empathy are the cornerstones of good intimate relationships, providing the safest, most rewarding place for a person to grow and flourish.

You have to invest in the growth of your partner with tolerance, support, and acceptance, just as he or she must do the same for you in order to grow the relationship and your individual Selves. If either of you only focuses on your "I" and you resist your mate's self-expression and independence or he does yours, you will live to resent each other, and eventually push the other person out of your life.

This means you must learn to accept and tolerate your mate's behavior from a place of strength and self-confidence, to understand the meaning behind the behavior, and to appreciate its importance in your relationship. By this I don't mean passive acceptance of bad behavior, nor am I suggesting that you are powerless to confront your partner. What I'm referring to is a more global regard for the value of your mate and his or her overall importance to you and to your partnership, despite the dysfunctional manifestations of the past that both of you bring to the relationship.

"You have to invest in the growth of your partner with tolerance, support, and acceptance, just as he or she must do the same for you in order to grow the relationship and your individual Selves."

What would this form of acceptance look like in Judy and Ken's interaction? In lieu of responding to their differences with polarizing responses ("You have a way of ruining my excitement about the things I love most," "I can't win. You're so sensitive about these things, Judy"), imagine if Ken and Judy recognized each other's past hurts, understood the other's intimacy needs, and shifted their attitudes to having greater tolerance and understanding in the larger perspective of their relationship.

Once a mutually supportive view of "we" is developed and used as the framework to resolve differences, mutual respect and positive change are much more likely to take place.

Acceptance also means relinquishing the hurtful strategies couples learned from their childhood dysfunction and use when they are attempting to resolve their differences. These include guilt-tripping, threats, blaming, withdrawing support and nurturing, hints of abandonment, and discounting a partner's needs.

But bear in mind, no matter how accepting you are or how well you turn away from hurtful strategies, conflict won't go away. It's inevitable between intimate partners, and it's okay—in fact necessary—for two independent "I's" to want different things. Each partner's needs are equally valid. Your need for closeness is as important as your partner's need for space. Your love of intellectual dialogue is as important as your partner's love of sports. Conflict must be solved together as partners. Resorting to guilt-tripping or threats or lack of support creates winners and losers, not partners. Remember, you are players on the same team at all times and the burden for solutions is on both of you.

Without that team approach, you and your partner will not feel heard or safe and will likely respond to the other in defensive, aggressive, and critical ways. So begin disagreements by bearing in mind the overall value of the "we." Mutual acceptance, which emphasizes differences rather than deficits between you and your partner, begets mutual change. This leads to a haven for your "we" and promotes enhanced intimacy.

Exercise 4: Where Was the "We"?

One way of exploring the ways in which you can forge a compatible "we" while honoring the two individuals within a relationship is to look at how this was done or not done in your former marriage. This exercise can provide insights into the places you honored your relationship as an entity in and of itself, and where you needed to accept and support one another as individuals with differing needs:

Answer the following questions as honestly as possible:

1. When your marital relationship grew out of the "honeymoon phase," what things did you notice about your partner that you were not entirely happy with? In some cases, these may be things you found endearing initially—the way he slurped his spaghetti, the hours she spent finding the perfect outfit, his love of getting together with the guys to cheer on their favorite team, her way of stringing out a story at a dinner party and never getting the punch line quite right.

2. Looking back at the things you nitpicked over, what would you change about those arguments if you could turn back time? Would you ignore your partner's quirks more often, try to figure out what was behind that behavior, modify your own behavior when your spouse complained about something minor, laugh instead of nag or sigh?

3. Identify those things you know bothered your partner about you. Would you change them, explain why they were important to you, involve your spouse to make him or her feel a part of your life, find a friend or relative to share those things with instead of your spouse?

4. Some of your quirks are just a part of who you are, and you don't want to let go of them. What do you wish your spouse had been more tolerant of? How could he or she have shown this acceptance in a loving way?

As this exercise shows subtly, the most successful marriages are those created by two well-formed, secure individuals who come together for the purpose of enhancing one another. This model is in contrast to one that is used too frequently, where spouses seek out marriage to complete their identity, and when they fail, turn to divorce. It's not your partner's responsibility to define you or even to provide you with happiness. You must learn to do those for yourself.

Chapter 8

The Importance of Individual Counseling

Divorce is one of the most stressful passages of life a person will go through, second only to the death of a loved one, and sometimes just as hard. The grief over this loss will oftentimes leave divorced individuals awash in fear, anger, guilt, grief, shame, loss of identity, and the diminished capacity to cope with the ordinary demands of life. Divorce closes one chapter of life and starts a new one, putting individuals in places where they have never been before—and often never dreamed they'd be.

The healing process involves putting together a new and meaningful life. It doesn't happen overnight. Though it would be wonderful if healing from a divorce were like getting over the flu—rest, drink lots of fluids, and come out the other side good as new—surviving a divorce is much more like recovering from a traumatic accident in which you need to relearn basic tasks in order to thrive in a new, forever changed life.

Some people can do this on their own, depending on the magnitude of their post-divorce problems and how much support they have. But many need a helping hand, and that's nothing to be ashamed of. Think about having a bad toothache: Would you avoid going to the dentist only to have the pain grow worse, or would you find a doctor who could ease your suffering? Whether you are feeling the pain of a cavity or the grief of divorce, the earlier you get help, the more likely you can stop the hurt before it gets worse.

"Though it would be wonderful if healing from a divorce were like getting over the flu—rest, drink lots of fluids, and come out the other side good as new—surviving a divorce is much more like recovering from a traumatic accident in which you need to relearn basic tasks in order to thrive in a new, forever changed life."

Why Counseling?

People in the midst of divorce can feel rejected, abandoned, helpless, and fearful. As a soon-to-be non-partnered person, they can feel confused about their identity. A patient of mine, a successful, attractive woman in her forties, came into my office one day having learned that her husband was leaving her for another woman. The fear and anger she felt in the face of what, for her, was an unexpected and terrifying turn of events was palpable. "Why me?" she sobbed. "I was certain we loved each other. I supported him, in every sense of the word, throughout our twenty-two-year marriage. Our children are grown and have moved out. I have never lived alone. How am I going to make it on my own? I could just kill him for doing this to me."

"The intense problems, stressors, and emotions that divorcing people face, coupled with a need to talk about them to a supportive, solution-oriented professional, lead many to seek counseling—and rightly so."

This patient embodies some of the basic emotions that can overwhelm anyone in the midst of divorce. Some will experience these feelings at a more intense level than others. Some will have pre-existing emotional disorders that will be greatly exacerbated by the stress of divorce. In order to successfully navigate through this uncharted terrain, a counselor can be critical in helping manage anxiety, depression, fears, and overwhelming confusion.

The intense problems, stressors, and emotions that divorcing people face, coupled with a need to talk about them to a supportive, solution-oriented professional, lead many to seek counseling—and rightly so. Counseling provides people with the opportunity to speak to someone who listens, is supportive, and has tools and techniques designed to help clients cope with or improve their circumstances, strengthen their self-esteem, and promote change.

"No matter what warning signs you may be experiencing, a good point of reference is this: If you are questioning whether or not you need counseling, you probably do. Trust your instincts and reach out for help."

How Do I Know I Need a Counselor?

There many signs that signal the need for outside help. Reactions to divorce and grief vary, but if you are experiencing any of the following, you should consider meeting with a counselor.

- *Depression* – If you feel a prolonged sense of sadness, uneasiness, or anxiety that you just can't seem to shake, clinical depression may be the cause. Your counselor can determine whether or not your depression is a normal part of the grieving process and a natural response to the many losses you are experiencing or is due to other causes. This is an important distinction, as the course of treatment may vary.

- *Self-Doubt or Low Self-Esteem* – No matter how successful, intelligent, or accomplished you are, how much money you make or how beautiful you look, self-doubt or low self-esteem can set in after a divorce and rob you of your feelings of self-worth.

- *Difficulty Concentrating on Day-to-Day Life* – If you are having difficulty focusing at work, giving your full attention to your children, or participating in friendships, the pain you feel over your divorce may be drowning out important aspects of your life.

- *Obsession with the Divorce* – Many of my patients come to me obsessing about what went wrong with their marriage, who was at fault, and how unfair the situation is. While all of that may be true, excessive preoccupation with the dissolution of your marriage will not help you move forward to a better situation.

- *Persistent Anger* – In some cases, the grief and loss that happens as the result of a divorce expresses itself as persistent anger and aggression, not only toward an ex-spouse, but in response to the world in general. Often, this anger masks underlying feelings such as sadness, fear, or anxiety. It is important that a professional counselor identifies the defensive anger and helps you access the grief reaction that is necessary for your healing.

- *Confusion* – If you find yourself having difficulty thinking clearly, making decisions, or even knowing where to begin in order to move on with life, a counselor can help you sort things out and get on track.

- *Inability to Plan for the Future* – When you were married, you may have taken for granted what the future held. Divorce erases that future, and many people feel at a loss to redefine it.

- *Substance Abuse Problems, Sleeping Disorders, Risk-Taking, and Other Addictions* – It is common to dull the pain of divorce with alcohol, drugs, sex, and a host of other addictive behaviors. But soon the escape can turn into an extension of your problems. A skilled counselor can assist you to identify your compulsive behavior and, if necessary, refer you to a specialist who can help "wean" you. Typically, this rehab process must happen first, paving the way for you to access your underlying grief feelings.

No matter what warning signs you may be experiencing, a good point of reference is this: If you are questioning whether or not you need counseling, you probably do. Trust your instincts and reach out for help.

———————————————

"When looking to a friend or family member for support, it is important to understand the difference between speaking to them as opposed to a counselor: one is bound by the constraints of their close relationship to you, the other is a neutral party."

———————————————

Talking to a Friend or Family Member vs. Talking to a Counselor

Having a supportive network of friends and family to help you through your divorce is very important during this traumatic time. The people who love you and know you best can offer a shoulder to cry on, words of encouragement, reminders of your strength and worth, and help with all those little things that make life easier, from watching the kids while you run errands to helping you find a new apartment or taking you out to lunch.

But friends and family provide a different kind of support than a divorce counselor is trained to give. When looking to a friend or family member for support, it is important to understand the difference between speaking to them as opposed to a counselor: one is bound by the constraints of their close relationship to you, the other is a neutral party. Some things to consider:

- **When you tell friends or family members about your conflict with your spouse, it is normal for them to want to take your side as a sign of support.** They may agree with you even when it's obvious that you mishandled your side of the conflict. A therapist will ally with you to help you see more clearly what your role was in the failed marriage. A good divorce counselor will help you create deep self-awareness that frees you to make changes.

- **Those who are closest to you may not be totally honest with you as a way of sparing your feelings.** A counselor doesn't want to hurt your feelings either, but he or she knows how to be straightforward and direct and how to say things in a way that won't be so painful. Therapists also know how to let a client go at his or her own pace, slowing things down when necessary to provide a safe space where he or she can reveal fears and concerns.

- **Friends and family members will see your situation through their own lens and offer you solutions that worked for them.** A counselor will help you come up with what is right for your own unique situation, without bias.

- **A defining characteristic of close personal relationships is that they are based on mutual support.** There is a natural expectation of reciprocation: you help me with my problems, I'll help you with yours; you share in my triumphs, I'll share in yours. Divorce counseling is about YOU. A counselor is not there to share his own past in order to look for solutions or congratulations. And in the aftermath of divorce, that focus on Self is exactly what you need.

- **When speaking to those you love about your fears, anger, pain, and worries, it's easy to feel that you are a burden.** The look on someone's face, a sigh, or even the advice that you need to "just get over it" can make you feel misunderstood, judged, or unsupported. A divorce therapist, however, wants to hear your "old" stories in order to identify underlying patterns and to professionally and nonjudgmentally bring them into your awareness. Once these patterns, both good and bad, have become a part of your consciousness, your counselor can help you process them in order to help you change and grow.

- **There are certain private issues that you may not feel comfortable talking about with friends or family:** sexual problems, physical or mental abuse, addictions, guilt, and so on. In supportive counseling, you should feel free to share all your concerns without being judged, knowing that this honesty is a part of the healing process that will help you move forward.

- **Even when you talk to those you care about most, there is no guarantee of confidentiality.** In divorce counseling, everything you express is kept in the strictest confidentiality and can only be released with the client's permission. Counseling can be very liberating when you know what you say to your counselor stays with your counselor.

- **People you look to for support, especially family, have influenced your developmental behaviors, and therefore aren't the best people to advise you on how to recognize and change those behaviors.** In fact, they may use the very same destructive behaviors in their interactions with others! A therapist, on the other hand, especially one who has studied the separation-individuation process as it pertains to marriage, has the professional tools and objective view to recognize shortcomings in your development and help you complete them.

As an analogy, if your car breaks down a friend may be able to help you change a tire, jump the battery, or add gas to an empty tank—all of which can be very helpful. But it isn't likely they can get under the hood and assess more serious damage. You need a knowledgeable mechanic to diagnose a critical problem, someone you know has the proper tools and experience to make the repairs. Think of a therapist as your mechanic—for your well-being as a strong, independent individual.

Divorce Counseling: What Is It and Where Did It Come From?

When looking for a therapist, you may wonder what sort of professional you should look for. Should you seek out a grief counselor, a family therapist, someone who has worked with couples, someone who only does individual counseling?

Today there are professional counselors like myself whose work focuses specifically on divorce. Like me, most have clients who are in all of the three phases of divorce: pre-divorce (debating whether to stay in the marriage or leave), divorce (in the midst of the legal process), or post-divorce (after the divorce is complete, when many individuals find themselves having trouble moving on).

Counseling in any or all of the three stages can help an individual explore the feelings and behaviors that contributed to his or her marital problems; think through issues around the legal divorce such as custody and visitation rights involving children, alimony or support, and division of property, as well as help regulate out-of-control feelings that might cause poor legal judgment; develop a stronger sense of Self; and of course manage the inevitable grief responses.

The field of divorce counseling is fairly new, since it is only in the last forty years or so that divorce has become an accepted institution in the United States. Prior to that time, divorced men and women were looked down upon, even labeled as sick or neurotic. Little was known about the emotional toll of divorce on the individual until it began to be studied more closely in the late 1970s and early 1980s, as more people sought divorce. Therapists began to combine their experiences with grief counseling and couples counseling to address this new group of people in need of help.

What they discovered was that the first year post-divorce is when the impact is most intense. But they also learned that healing from divorce takes time: typically a year for every five years of marriage. Yet individual experiences with divorce vary, just as experiences grieving the death of a loved one do.

In the 1980s, Ellyn Bader and Peter Pearson integrated developmental theory into marital therapy—a milestone in that field. I have taken their work one step further, integrating the earlier work of Margaret Mahler and her separation-individuation theory into therapy with divorcing individuals. In fact, it has become the conceptual framework of my counseling work.

My Form of Divorce Counseling

The two tasks that form the core of my divorce counseling are (1) mourning the loss of the relationship, your spouse, and the life you imagined for yourself as a married person, and (2) developing a stronger identity so you can move forward with a richer, more complete sense of self.

As I pointed out in Chapter 2, when it comes to grief, most people know very little about what to expect and how to handle the emotional turbulence they experience when they lose their partner to divorce. My job is to assist them in the process by helping them face their grief, which is essential to recovery, and when necessary identify the defenses that are impeding the process.

The second focus of my counseling is to promote growth by healing the problems that resulted from incomplete separation-individuation with the primary caregiver, a topic I discuss at length in Chapters 3–5. Though patients cannot re-create from memory the original mother-child experience, through a combination of carefully designed interventions and my theoretical knowledge of early development, in tandem with talk therapy, we can come to better understand the patient's past and developmental lapses that later contributed to problems in the marital relationship. I then help my patient develop his or her "I" through the counseling relationship—what I like to call "trying on developmental wings."

After helping my clients heal their developmental defects, I then aid in the development of their autonomy. This means encouraging them to arrive at their own solutions in contrast to my setting new goals for them. Mahler herself stressed that while the principal developmental achievements take place during the early months of life, the process is never complete. New phases introduce new directions. With each round there are new opportunities for growth and second chances. Thus we all have the opportunity to complete our development.

A unique part of my therapy is that I work with many of my clients over the phone. Historically, the telephone has been used for hotline counseling, crisis intervention, or as an adjunct to traditional therapy. I have taken that a step further by using the phone for ongoing therapy. It has proven to offer privacy and convenience for clients, and studies have shown that patients feel more at ease when they are in their own environment, where they are less inhibited or guarded about discussing difficult topics.

What to Look For in a Divorce Counselor

When most people decide to go into therapy, they have no idea what to look for in a therapist. Of primary importance is finding someone with whom you can have a good working relationship, a person you view as a safe, caring listener devoted to helping you heal and thrive. Here are some questions to ask yourself as you seek a counselor who is right for you.

- **Is she compassionate and caring?** Like a good parent, who is involved in a similar pursuit: supporting and encouraging the growth and development of her child, a therapist should be able to empathize with your pain, psychological issues, and other difficulties, without judgment.

- **Is he authentic?** It is important to feel at ease with your therapist. Does he communicate openly and directly, relate to you as a real person, make you feel comfortable?

- **Does she relate to you as an equal?** This does not mean your therapist is your friend; it means that you develop a respectful alliance as two individuals working toward a singular goal: your individual growth. Your therapist should never act arrogant, superior, or condescending toward you.

- **Is he able to help you face your emotional pain, not cover it up?** A primary goal of therapy is to actively engage your emotions in order to work through your pain. If your therapist shies away from this important task, you should look for another professional.

- **Is she emotionally stable?** A counselor should never let her own issues intrude on yours or affect her clinical judgment. She should be aware of her own emotional and relationship issues and have resolved them before attempting to help you do the same. A good therapist is introspective and self-aware.

- **Does he act as a role model?** A good divorce counselor relates to others in a respectful and compassionate way, modeling the ability to regulate feelings and behavior as well as an interest in self-exploration—all goals of therapy.

- **Does she have a good understanding of the legal as well as the emotional aspects of divorce?** The transition from being part of a couple to being successfully divorced has as much to do with exercising emotional intelligence as it does legal intelligence. In order for your therapist to address the many challenges you face, she should understand both aspects clearly.

- **Does he tailor his counseling to you as an individual?** Your therapist should provide skills, advice, tools, and exercises unique to you and your situation. If it feels as though he is trying to fit you into a theoretical framework that doesn't suit your situation, he may not be the right person for you.

- **Does she allow you to come to your own conclusions rather than telling you what to do and how to live your life?** A counselor should offer tools to help you

strengthen your own decision-making abilities.
If she is directing the way you live your life,
see that as a red flag.

How to Evaluate Progress in Counseling

Once you have made the leap, found the right therapist, and begun counseling, there are several questions you can ask yourself on a continuing basis to measure your progress. Keep in mind that you can't just open the door to change and run through it. This process takes time. These questions will help you evaluate where you stand:

1. Is your life changing for the better (at work, at home, socially)?

2. Are you meeting the goals you and your counselor set?

3. Is counseling challenging you and stretching you beyond your comfort zone?

4. Do you understand yourself better?

5. Do you feel more confident and stronger in your ability to take charge of your own life as a single person?

6. Are your relationships improving? Are you able to incorporate new behaviors into your relationships that are improved substitutes for the negative behaviors that contributed to the marriage failure?

You may find it valuable to keep a journal of this journey. Reading back to where you were when you started will show you that you are on the right path, or what you need to tweak. Though each person experiences the breakup of a marriage in his or her own way, the following case study exemplifies the steps many people follow as they move from the upheaval of divorce to a place of independence and strength. Reading it will help you measure where you were, where you are, and where you're going on your own deeply personal journey.

Joyce's Story

Like each of you in the act of transitioning through the divorce process, my client, Joyce, had little idea how to respond to the demands of single life. Suddenly single—not of her own choosing—after forty-one years of marriage to Jim, and having just completed construction on the home they were to retire to now that their three children were grown and out of the house, she wondered, *Now what?* The one thing she was certain of was that the foundation upon which her life had rested needed major reorganization.

When Joyce first sought my help she was, understandably, in the throes of an emotional crisis. In Chapter 2, we talked of the complex upheaval of emotions that make up grief, a normal reaction to divorce. Joyce's emotions fluctuated between loving and detesting Jim, unbearable sadness, relief at being unburdened of his angry outbursts and slothful, irresponsible, and unhealthy lifestyle, and unspeakable loneliness.

During our early counseling sessions, I was never quite sure what array of emotions would rise to the surface. Joyce was baffled by the fact that she even gave Jim a second thought; after all, he had left her for another woman, proclaiming that he "just wanted to be happy." By Joyce's account Jim treated her in an aloof, insensitive, and emotionally abusive way throughout the marriage. Although she recognized she was not a perfect partner, her perception of her role as Jim's wife was that she was gentle, kind, and never made him feel like less of a man. Moreover, as an executive and the higher earner of the two, she paid for all of his toys.

We know that although divorce severs marital and social ties with your partner, it does not dissolve emotional ties. Therefore, my primary role during the early stages of Joyce's acute grief was to encourage her to express the myriad confusing and often contradictory feelings she was experiencing. I needed to continuously remind her that avoiding those feelings would thwart her goal of self-renewal. These reminders were particularly important for Joyce because she described herself as someone who buries her feelings and can "busy myself like a mouse on a wheel, creating a lot of noise in my head" to detach from the pain.

Typical of those who have masterminded their divorce because they have someone waiting in the wings, Jim was farther along in the process of letting go than Joyce was. Nevertheless, as the intensity of her grief subsided, an interesting shift took place. She determined that she did not want to remain stuck in a life of hate and anger, indefinitely mourning the loss of her marriage and blaming Jim for her misery. Although this was a crucial revelation, Joyce was unsure what to replace those feelings with.

As her negative feelings and identity as a married woman dissipated, Joyce found herself in a position to tackle what she described as "the challenge of being independent and the struggle to be alone." Joyce was very confused by the fact that although in her professional life she was regarded as a self-assured woman very capable of making high-level business decisions, facing her personal life as a single woman gripped her with fear.

In order for Joyce to understand why she did not feel the same confidence when it came to making positive things happen in her personal life, I suggested that she needed to take a deep look at the self-defeating behaviors she had exhibited in the marriage, and the psychological cost she was paying for blaming that failed marriage entirely on Jim.

Let's turn for a moment to Joyce's primary family and the impact her early relationships had on her psychological development. Joyce was the oldest of five girls. For different reasons, her parents were unable to nurture her. Her mom was an alcoholic and drank heavily during Joyce's youth. Her dad was hospitalized with a rare disease when she was six years old, and later died, having never come home from the hospital. As the oldest child, Joyce assumed the gravity of her family situation with a hyper-responsible approach. She learned to manage her home environment with the skill of an adult, taking on a maternal role.

The chaotic home in which she grew up coupled with Joyce's lack of parental guidance led the young girl to have very low expectations of others, a worldview that lasted into adulthood and impacted her choice of Jim as a life partner. In the early stages of their relationship, Jim had been paternal toward her. According to Joyce, "He made me feel safe and protected." However, as Jim's alcoholism progressed (a situation Joyce conveniently turned her back on), he became less responsible financially and as a co-parent. And so Joyce found herself once again in a home life that to her felt "normal" but in fact revolved around family dysfunction.

With the weight of the world on her shoulders, working full-time with little help from her husband and struggling to be the best parent she knew how, Joyce continued down the road of being externally focused. Although Joyce was a stellar worker—just as she'd been an all-A student—and took impeccable care of her surroundings, she blamed herself mercilessly when she could not fix the problems at home.

As we can see, Joyce lacked control over her own life. There was precious little time available for her to consider her needs, her feelings, and her sense of Self. Similar to the childlike way she had secured love and approval from her mom by being the little caretaker, with Jim she became the perfect parent—not only to their children, but also to him. She made up for his deficits, took care of him when he was not taking care of himself, made excuses for him at work, and jumped in to rescue him whenever he needed rescuing. In short, a powerful co-dependency had developed between Joyce and Jim.

This unhealthy partnership continued for many years until Jim decided that he no longer needed Joyce to micromanage him. Indeed, he began to feel an overwhelming desire to detach from what he perceived as Joyce's controlling behavior. Having no insight into his role in the toxic dependency that he and Joyce had mutually developed, Jim decided to "become independent" of her by being with a less-controlling woman. It was at this point that he asked Joyce for a divorce.

It is not difficult to understand why Joyce had little sense of how to take care of herself. In our first counseling session, she stated painfully that she did not realize how much of her identity was wrapped up in being Jim's wife. Beyond what she did for others, she hardly had a clue what her value was.

Our work together was crystal clear. As an unattached woman who was grieving the loss of her life with her husband, Joyce had to develop new boundaries and a stronger sense of her Self. Only by putting a microscope on her early maternal relationship, its strengths and its deficits, was she able to understand her choice of Jim as her husband, how underdeveloped she was at the onset of her marriage, and ultimately how her immaturity contributed to its failure.

A year has passed since we began our counseling work together. Joyce sold her home and moved to a new city to be nearer to her three adult children. She decided to leave the executive life behind, and instead is volunteering her time to the needs of her community as well as to her adult children and their families. While Joyce is still struggling to successfully be on her own, she now recognizes that Jim was not a good partner and is experiencing a renewed sense of freedom as a non-partnered woman. She has begun dating. And as a direct result of the challenges she is embracing, in lieu of her primary focus on meeting the needs of others, she is learning how to value her Self.

Epilogue

One day after a gym class, shortly after my divorce was final, I found myself talking to a good friend whose husband had also recently left her for another woman. She, like me, was in the throes of a divorce. Linda, a hard-core runner who began training in the 1970s, suggested we run the Marine Corps Marathon in Washington D.C. that spring. I laughed and said that although I was in reasonably good shape, I probably couldn't even run one block. And yet, within seconds and without much forethought, I heard myself saying, "Sure, why not?"

Training was hard work. At first I struggled, wondering how on earth I would make it beyond a mile or two. But slowly, over weeks and months, I grew stronger. Soon I was running five, then ten, then fifteen miles. I told myself I would never stop persevering, never give up, never surrender. No matter how bad it got, no matter how deep the pain, the only way I could succeed was with persistence, faith in myself, and an unbreakable spirit. When I crossed the finish line that November, my sense of accomplishment and self-empowerment fed my wounded sense of Self and made me feel whole again.

Living through divorce is much like running a marathon. Whether you are an athlete in training or recovering from the shock of divorce, you will likely experience every conceivable emotion as you respond to the demands of the situation. Divorce, like running, drains you, challenges you, and at times you just want to sit down at the side of the road and give up. Yet divorce provides you with the ideal opportunity for personal discovery and development. There is a life waiting for you at the finish line, and you will complete this race a different person than the one who started it. If you refuse to move when the starting pistol is fired, you'll get nowhere. If you complete the race, this difficult path has taught you something: you have it within you to grow and change.

I hope that this book has helped you realize that you can alter your own course. Though it may feel like your past may forever define you, it is what you do with the past that truly matters. Look deeply. Learn to understand yourself. Learn to love who you are, who you were, and who you can be. Then step up to the starting line.

I know you can finish this race, and in the process redefine yourself in ways you never imagined.

About the Author

As a twin, creating an individual identity was always a challenge for Dr. Deborah Potashnik Hecker. From an early age, she was aware that without a clear sense of who you are, you will forever be dependent on others for what you lack in yourself. The study of psychology and counseling offered the ideal platform for her to learn about how we develop the Self. From her graduate training at Columbia University and The Union Institute (Cincinnati, Ohio) to her thirty-five years of clinical work and private practice, as well as her personal divorce journey, Dr. Hecker has the experience and wisdom to guide and inspire others to know themselves.

Additionally, she is trained in psychoanalysis, mediation, collaborative practice, and grief recovery. Dr. Hecker's individually tailored counseling has helped countless people face their challenges and build successful lives. She has appeared on many TV and radio shows, and has published numerous articles. For more information on Dr. Hecker and her practice, visit her website at www.DrDeborahHecker.com.

References

Chapter 1: Why Marriages Fail

Amato, Paul, and Denise Prevati. "People's Reasons for Divorcing: Gender, Social Class, the Life Course, and Adjustment." *Journal of Family Issues* 24, no. 5 (July 2003): 602–626.

Belluck, Pam. "To Avoid Divorce, Move to Massachusetts." *The New York Times.* November 14, 2004. www.nytimes.com/2004/11/14/weekinreview/14pamb.html.

Buri, John. "Love Bytes." *Psychology Today.* April 28, 2009. www.psychologytoday.com/blog/love-bytes/200904/ why-marriages-fail-part-1.

Centers for Disease Control and Prevention. *National Vital Statistics Reports* 58, no. 25 – Births, Marriages, Divorces, and Deaths: Provisional Data for 2009.

Cohn, Steven. "Why Second Marriages Fail." n.d. www.marriage-and-relationship-counseling.com/why-second-marriages-fail.html.

Diehl, Steve. "Why Marriages Fail." April 14, 2009. www.seeoursite.org/friends/whymarriagesfail.htm.

Divorcekit.com. "Top 10 Reasons Why Marriages Fail." n.d. www.divorcekit.com/marriages-fail.htm.

Granat, Jay. "Why Do Second or Third Marriages Fail?" June 10, 2010. www.northjersey.com/community/family/ reflections/96027209_Why_do_second_or_third_ marriages_seem_to_fail_.html.

Hecker, Deborah. "Guiding Your Clients through the
Emotional Turmoil of Dividing Assets."
www.drdeborahhecker.com.

Niolon, Richard. "Infidelity." *PsychPage*. October 1, 2011.
www.psychpage.com/family/library/infidelity.html.

Paul, Pamela. *The Starter Marriage and the Future of
Matrimony.* New York: Villard, 2002.

"Why Do People Get Divorced?" *PsychPage: Relationship
Reasons for Divorce.* n.d. www.psychpage.com/family/
mod_couples_thx/divorce.html.

Triplett, Gillis. "Why Do So Many Marriages Fail?"
August 15, 2001. www.gillistriplett.com/rel101/
articles/marriages_fail.html.

Chapter 2: The Importance of Grief to Post-Divorce Healing

Bonanno, George. *The Other Side of Sadness: What the New
Science of Bereavement Tells Us About Life After Loss.*
New York: Basic Books, 2009.

Grief Recovery Institute. www.grief-recovery.com.

Hecker, Deborah. "The Invaluable and Crucial Roles of
Mental Health Professionals in the Divorce Process."
www.drdeborahhecker.com.

James, John, and Russell Friedman. *The Grief Recovery
Handbook: The Action Program for Moving Beyond Death,
Divorce, and Other Losses.* New York: William Morrow,
2009.

———. "The Myth of the Stages of Dying, Death and Grief." *Skeptic.* June 22, 2008.

Neimeyer, Robert A. *Meaning Reconstruction and the Experience of Loss.* Washington, DC: American Psychological Association, 2001.

Trafford, Abigail. *Crazy Time: Surviving Divorce and Building a New Life.* New York: Harper Perennial, 1992.

Chapter 3: Childhood Identity Formation

Bader, Ellyn, and Peter T. Pearson. *In Quest of the Mythical Mate: A Developmental Approach to Diagnosis and Treatment in Couples Therapy.* Florence, KY: Brunner/Mazel, 1988.

Glenn, Marti, Jaelline Jaffe, and Jeanne Segal. "Parenting: Attachment, Bonding and Reactive Attachment Disorder." HealingResources.info. n.d. http://healingresources.info/children_attachment.htm.

Kaplan, Louise J. *Oneness and Separateness: From Infant to Individual.* New York: Touchstone, 1978.

Levine, Madeline. *Teach Your Children Well: Parenting for Authentic Success.* New York: Harper, 2012.

Mahler, Margaret, Fred Pine, and Anni Bergman. *The Psychological Birth of the Human Infant: Symbiosis and Individuation.* New York: Basic Books, 1975.

Perry, Bruce. "Bonding and Attachment in Maltreated Children: Consequences of Emotional Neglect in

Childhood." n.d. http://teacher.scholastic.com/
professional/bruceperry/bonding.htm.

**Chapter 4: Underdeveloped Identity and the Divorce-
Prone Relationship**

Bader, Ellyn, and Peter T. Pearson. *In Quest of the Mythical
Mate: A Developmental Approach to Diagnosis and
Treatment in Couples Therapy.* Florence, KY:
Brunner/Mazel, 1988.

Bergman, A. "From Psychological Birth to Motherhood:
The Treatment of an Autistic Child with Follow-up into
her Adult Life as a Mother." In *Parental Influences in
Health and Disease,* ed. E.J. Anthony and G. H. Pollock,
pp. 91–121. Boston: Little, Brown, 1985.

Levine, Amir, and Rachel S. F. Heller. *Attached: The New
Science of Adult Attachment and How It Can Help You
Find—and Keep—Love.* New York: Jerome P. Tarcher/
Penguin, 2010.

Weinhold, Barry K., and Janae Weinhold. *Breaking Free of
the Co-Dependency Trap*, rev. ed. Novato, Calif.:
New World Library, 2008.

Chapter 5: Developing the Underdeveloped "I"

Gunther, Randi. *Relationship Saboteurs: Overcoming the
Ten Behaviors That Undermine Love.* Oakland, Calif.:
New Harbinger Publications, 2010.

Weinhold, Barry K., and Janae Weinhold. *Breaking Free of
the Co-Dependency Trap*, rev. ed. Novato, Calif.:
New World Library, 2008.

Weinhold, Barry K., and Janae Weinhold. *The Flight From Intimacy: Healing Your Relationship of Counter-Dependency—the Other Side of Co-Dependency.* Novato, Calif.: New World Library, 2008.

Chapter 6: Taking the Steps Toward Change

Grohol, John. "15 Common Defense Mechanisms." http://psychcentral.com/lib/2007/15-common-defense-mechanisms/all/1/.

Mellody, Pia. *Facing CoDependence: What It Is, Where It Comes From, How It Sabotages Our Lives.* New York: HarperOne, 1989.

Mellody, Pia, and Andrea Wells Miller. *Breaking Free: A Recovery Workbook for Facing Codependence.* New York: HarperOne, 1989.

Prochaska, James O., John C. Norcross, and Carlo C. DiClemente. *Changing for Good: A Revolutionary Six-Stage Program for Overcoming Bad Habits and Moving Your Life Positively Forward.* New York: Harper, 1994.

Chapter 7: Characteristics of Healthy Intimacy: How to Remain Separate but Connected

Bagarozzi, Dennis A. *Enhancing Intimacy in Marriage: A Clinician's Guide.* New York: Brunner Routledge, 2001.

Hollis, James. *Finding Meaning in the Second Half of Life: How to Finally, Really Grow Up.* Toronto: New York: Gotham, 2006.

McKay, Matthew, Patrick Fanning, and Kim Paleg. *Couples Skills: Making Your Relationship Work*. Oakland, Calif.: New Harbinger, 2006.

Whitfield, Charles L. *Boundaries and Relationships: Knowing, Protecting, and Enjoying the Self*. Deerfield Beach, Fla.: Health Communications, 1993.

Chapter 8: The Importance of Individual Counseling

Blanck, Rubin, and Gertrude Blanck. *Marriage and Personal Development*. New York: Columbia University Press, 1968.

Edward, Joyce. "The Therapist as a Catalyst in Promoting Separation-Individuation." *Clinical Social Work Journal* 4, no. 3: 172–86.

Froiland, Donald J., and Thomas L. Hozeman. "Counseling for Constructive Divorce." *Personnel and Guidance Journal* 55, no. 9: 525–29.

Goldstein, Eda. *Object Relations Theory and Self Psychology in Social Work Practice*. New York: Free Press, 2002.

Wallerstein, Judith, and Joan Kelly. *Surviving the Breakup: How Children and Parents Cope with Divorce*. New York: Basic Books, 1996.